Tranquility

Coloring for Stress Relief and Relaxation

Tranquility

Coloring for Stress Relief and Relaxation
By Dina Criscione

A Very Special Thanks

I'd like to thank Pat Del Vecchio and the Entire Interventional Radiology Department team at The Miriam Hospital, Providence, RI. Without them none of this would be possible.

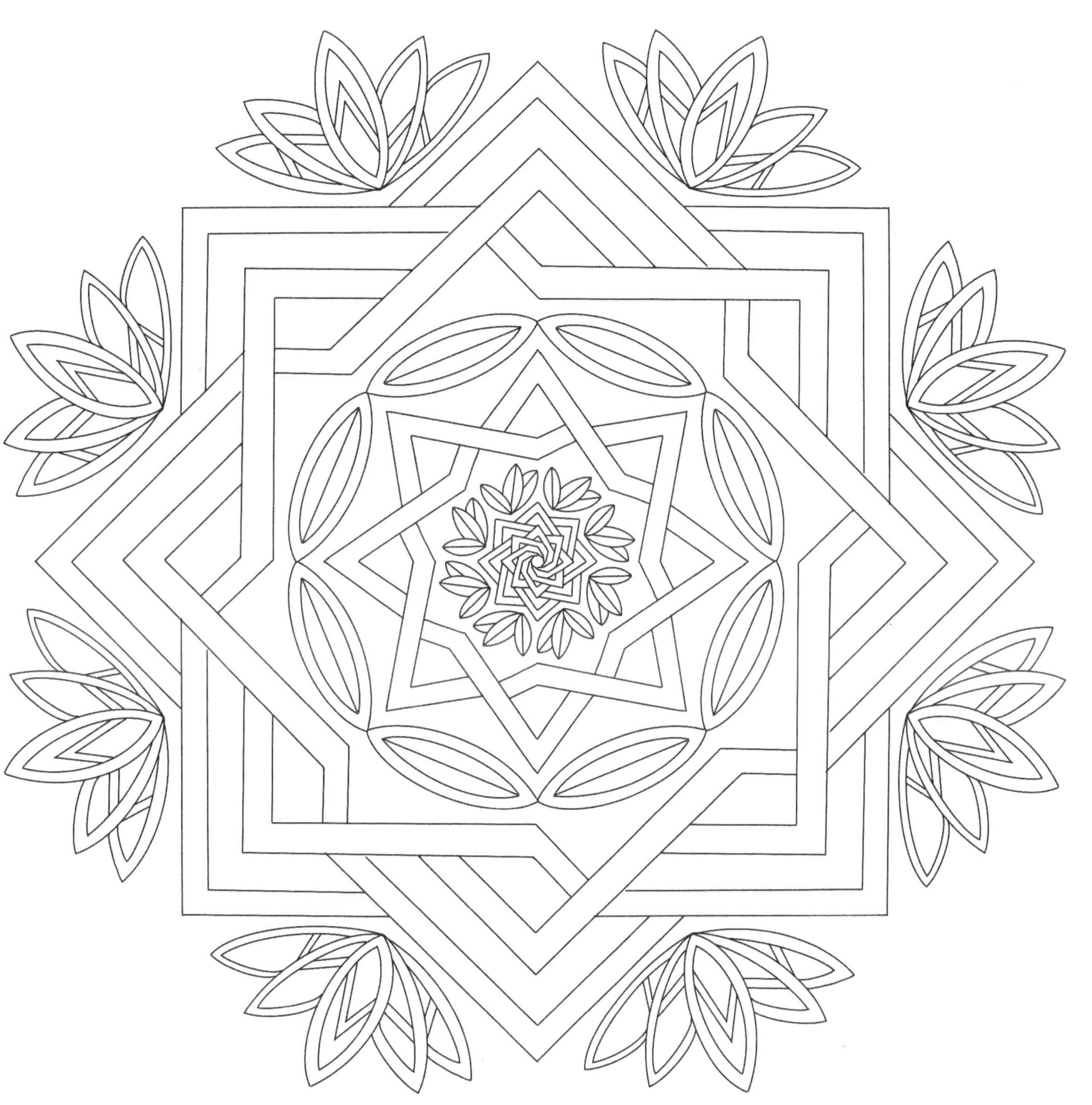

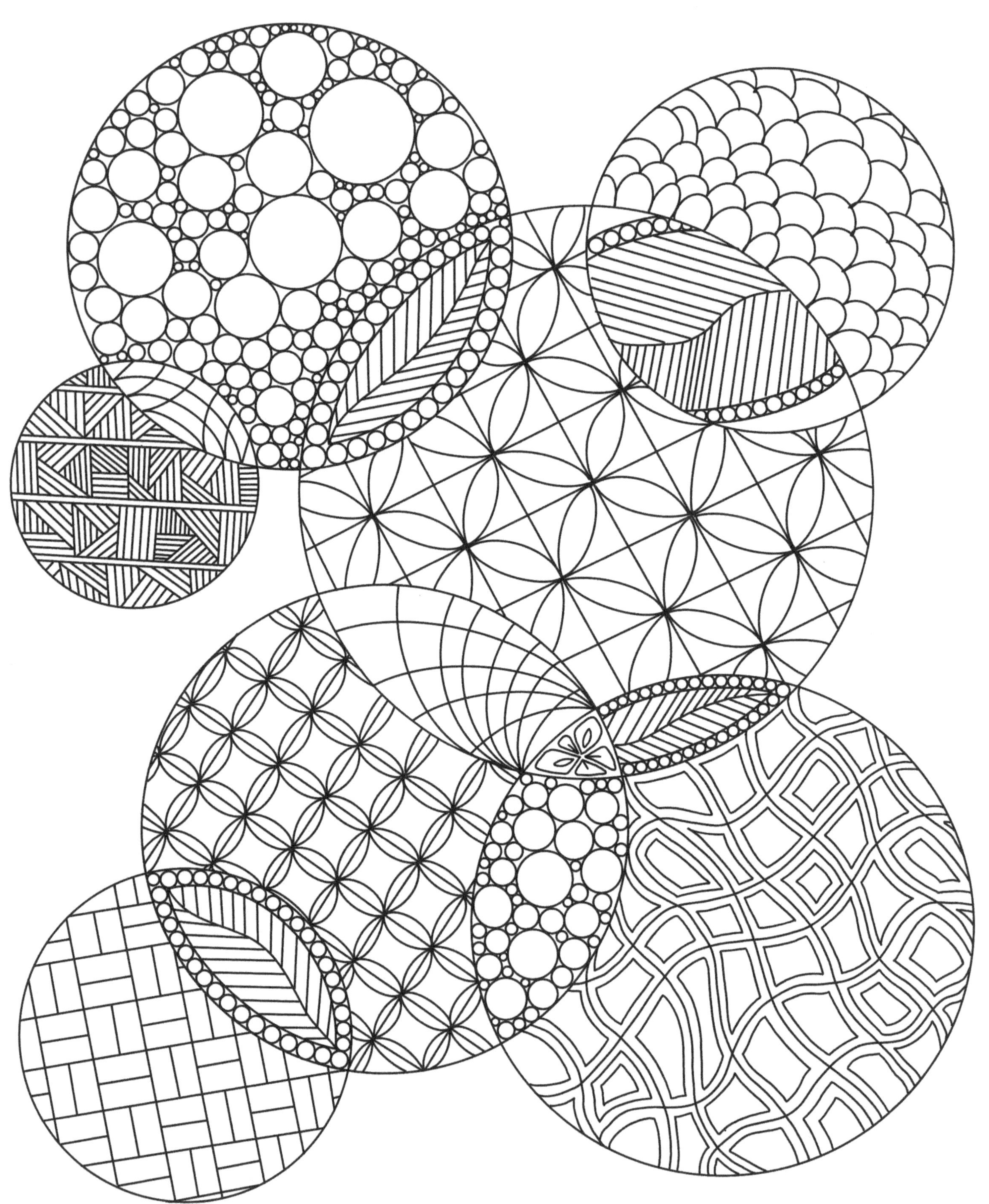

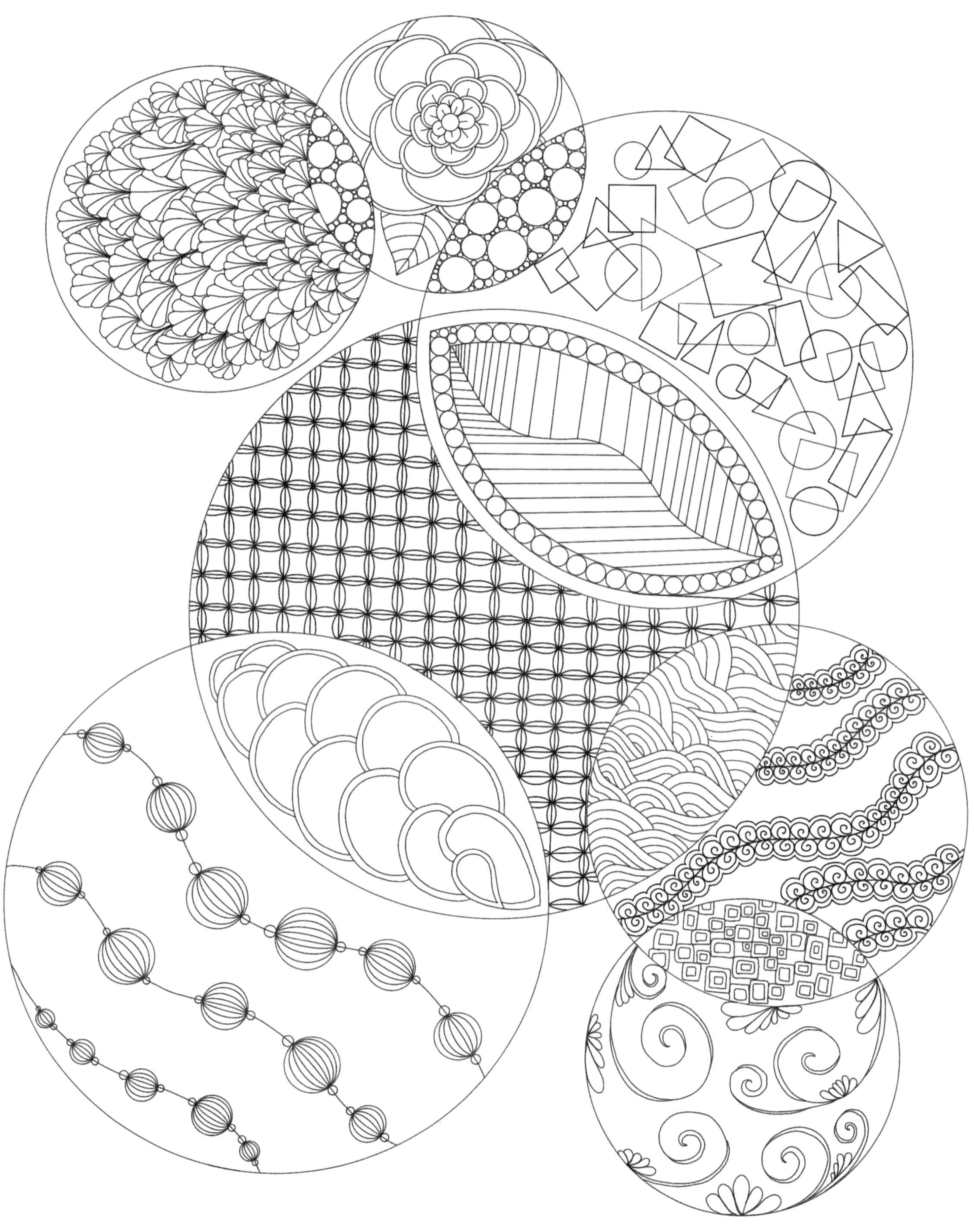

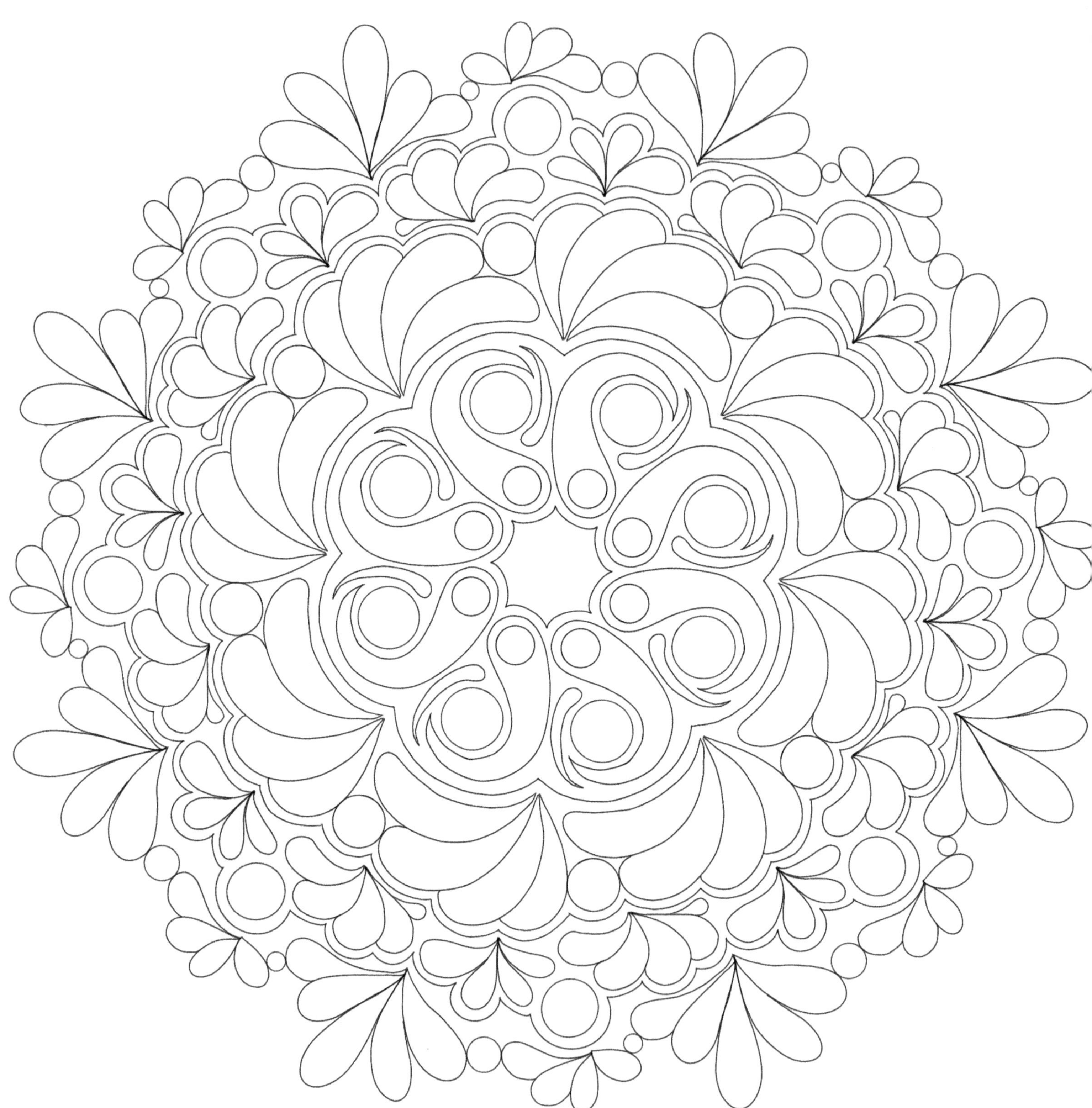

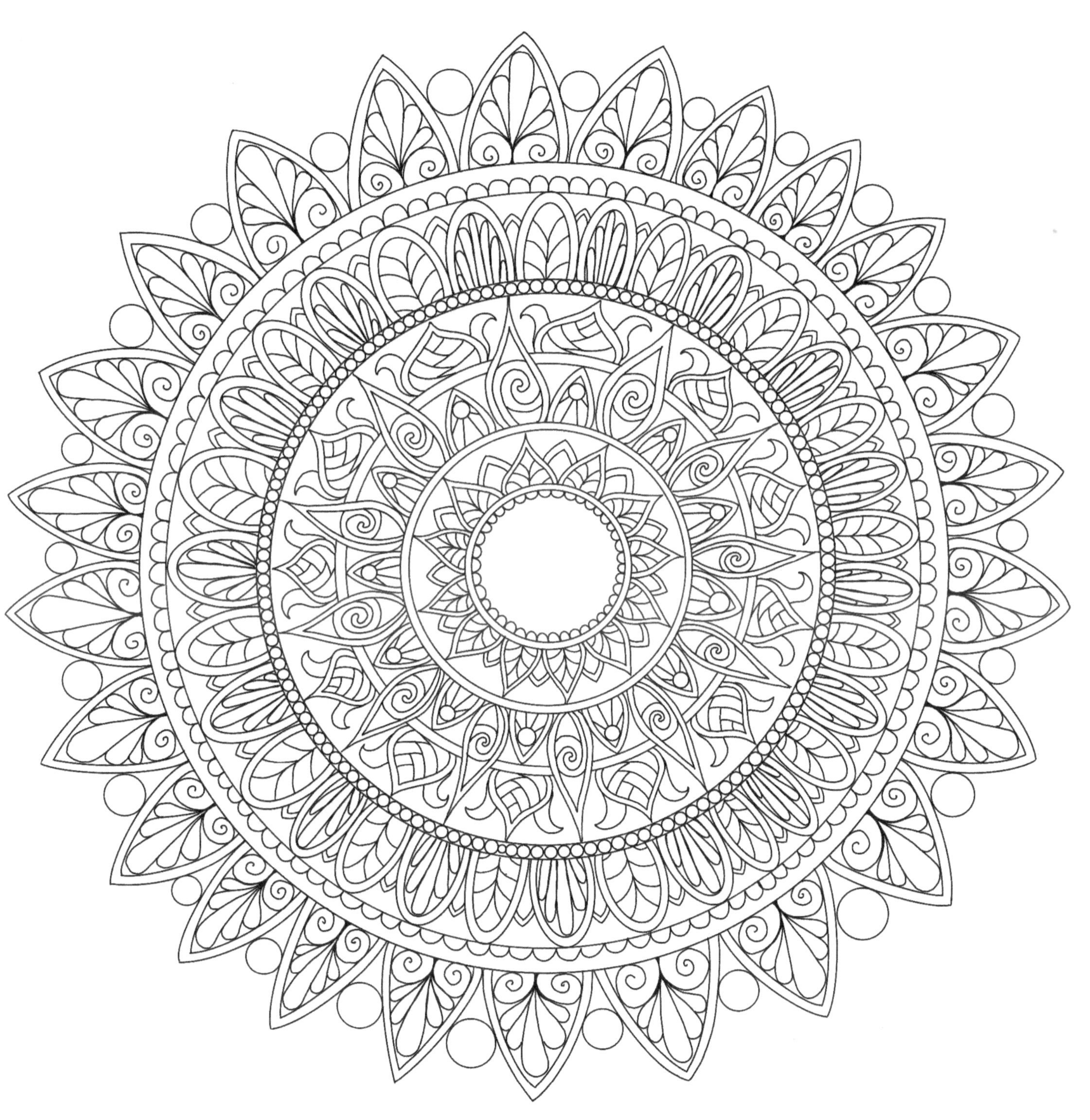

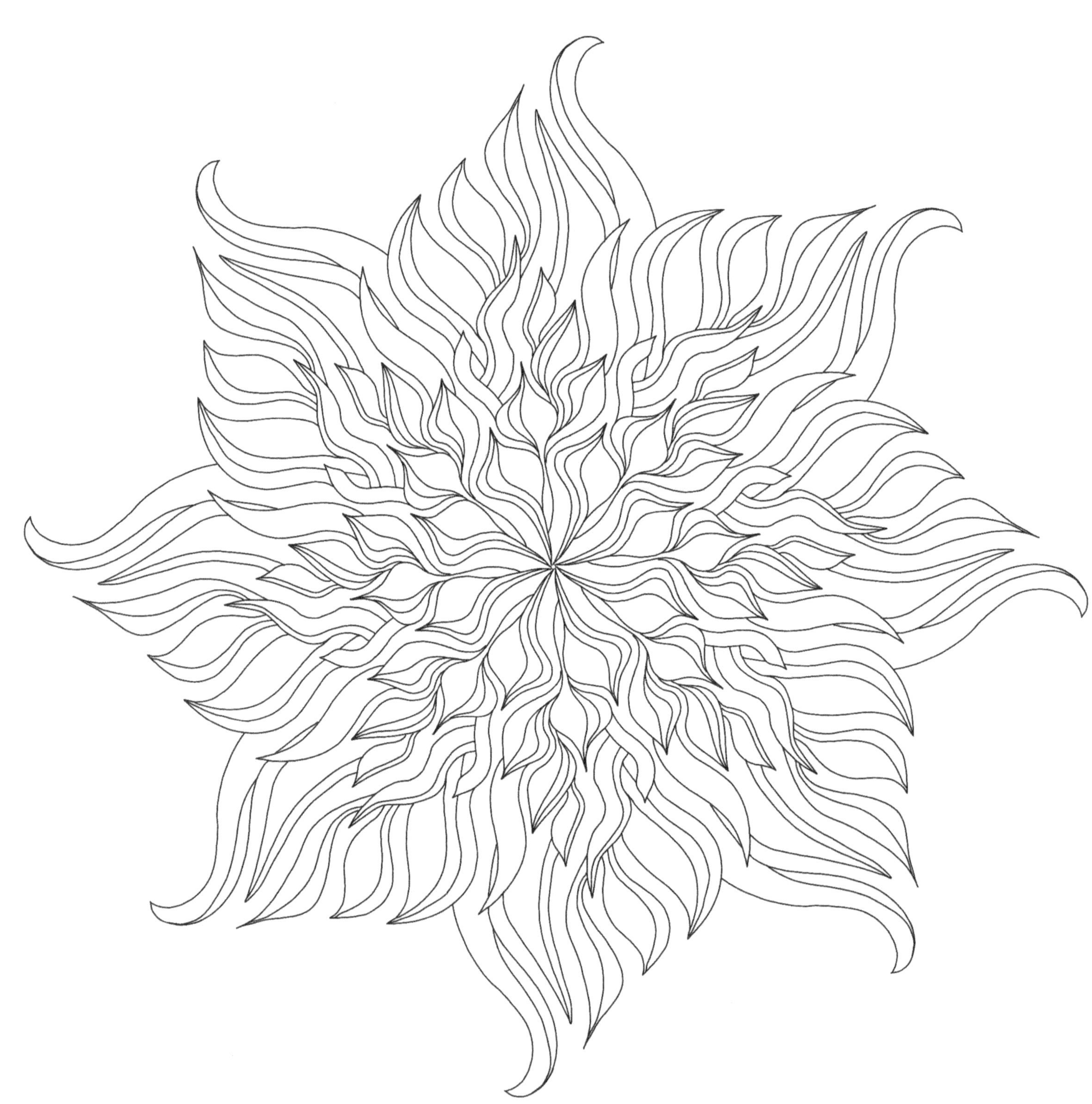

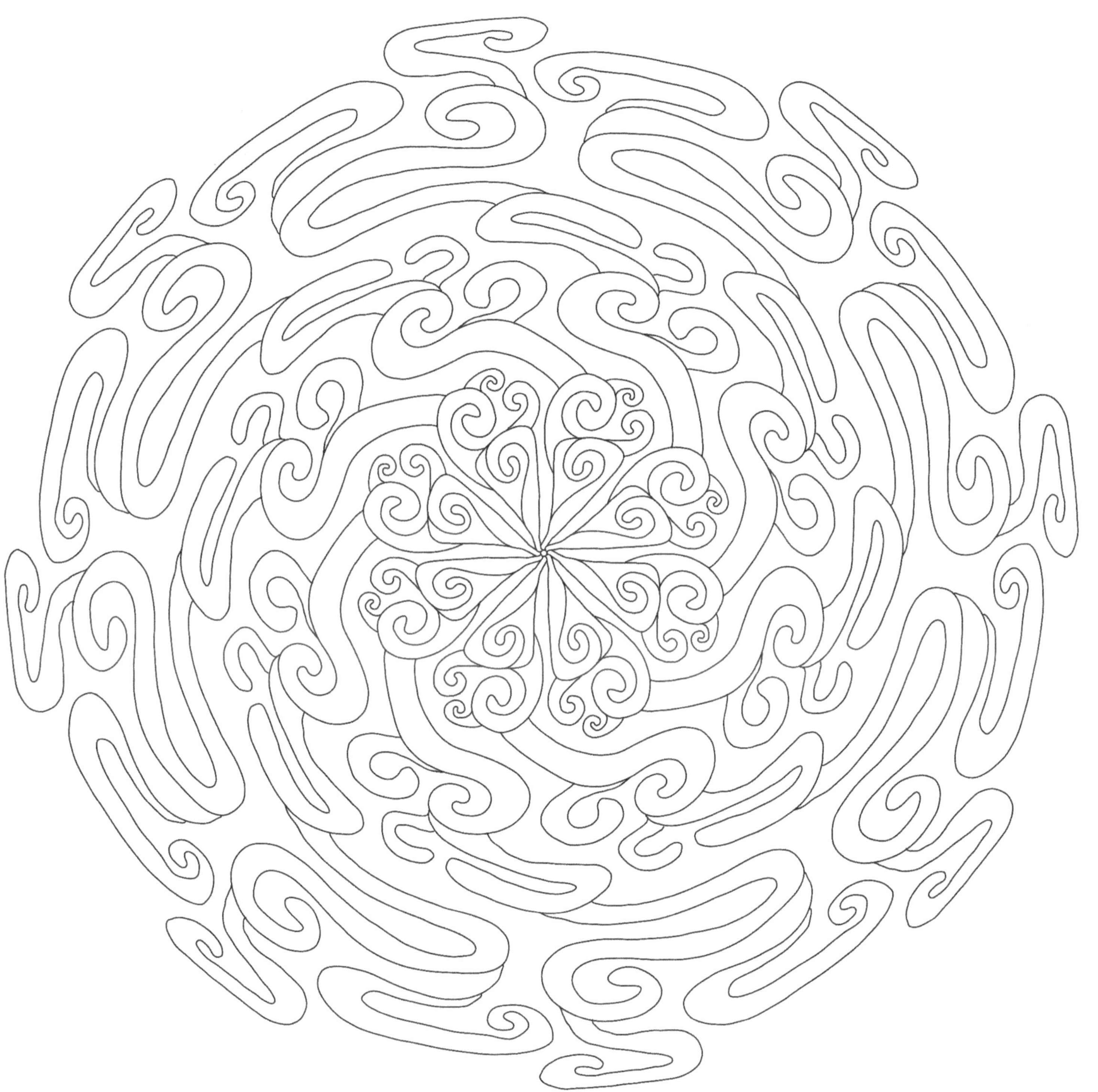

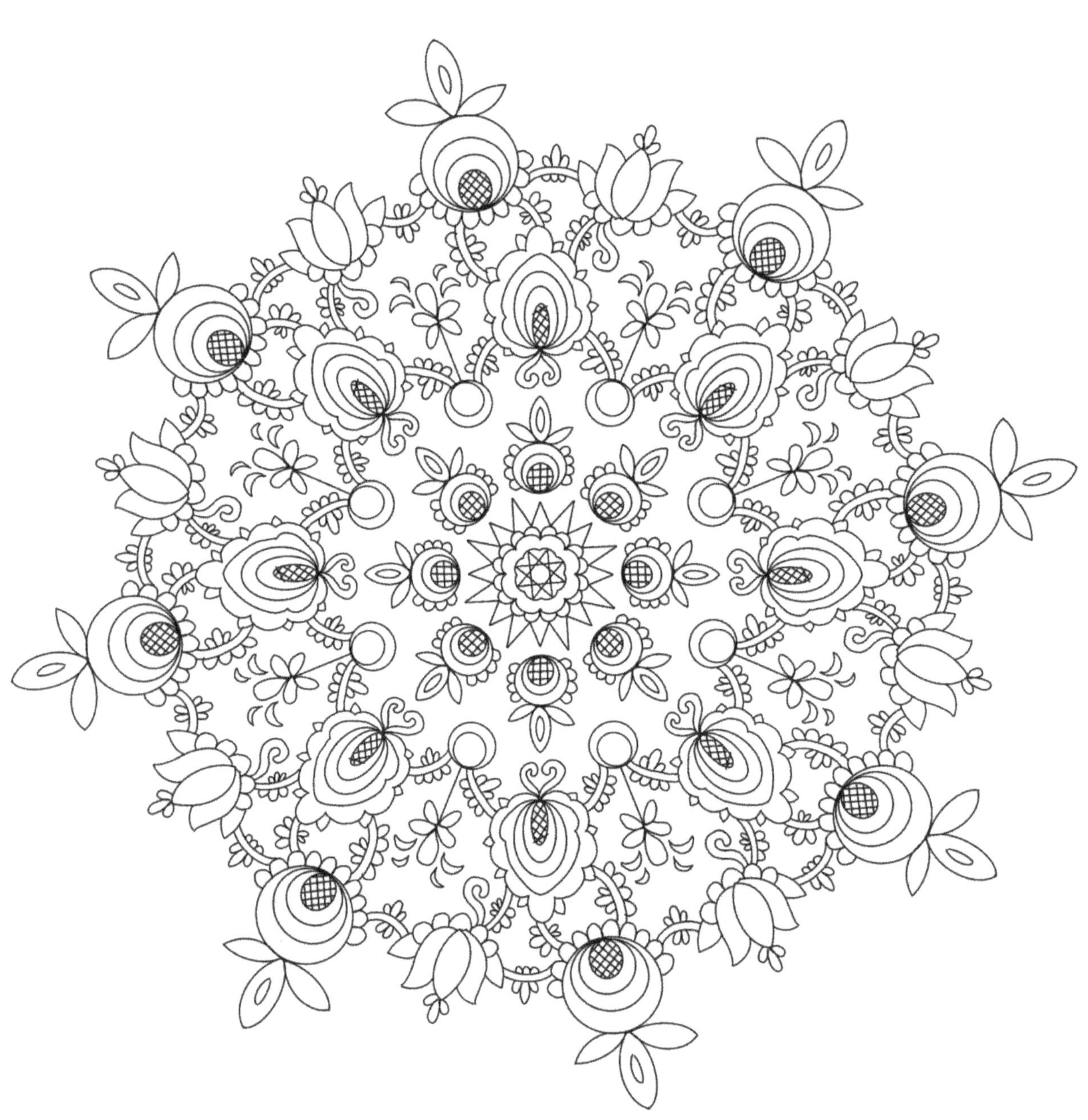

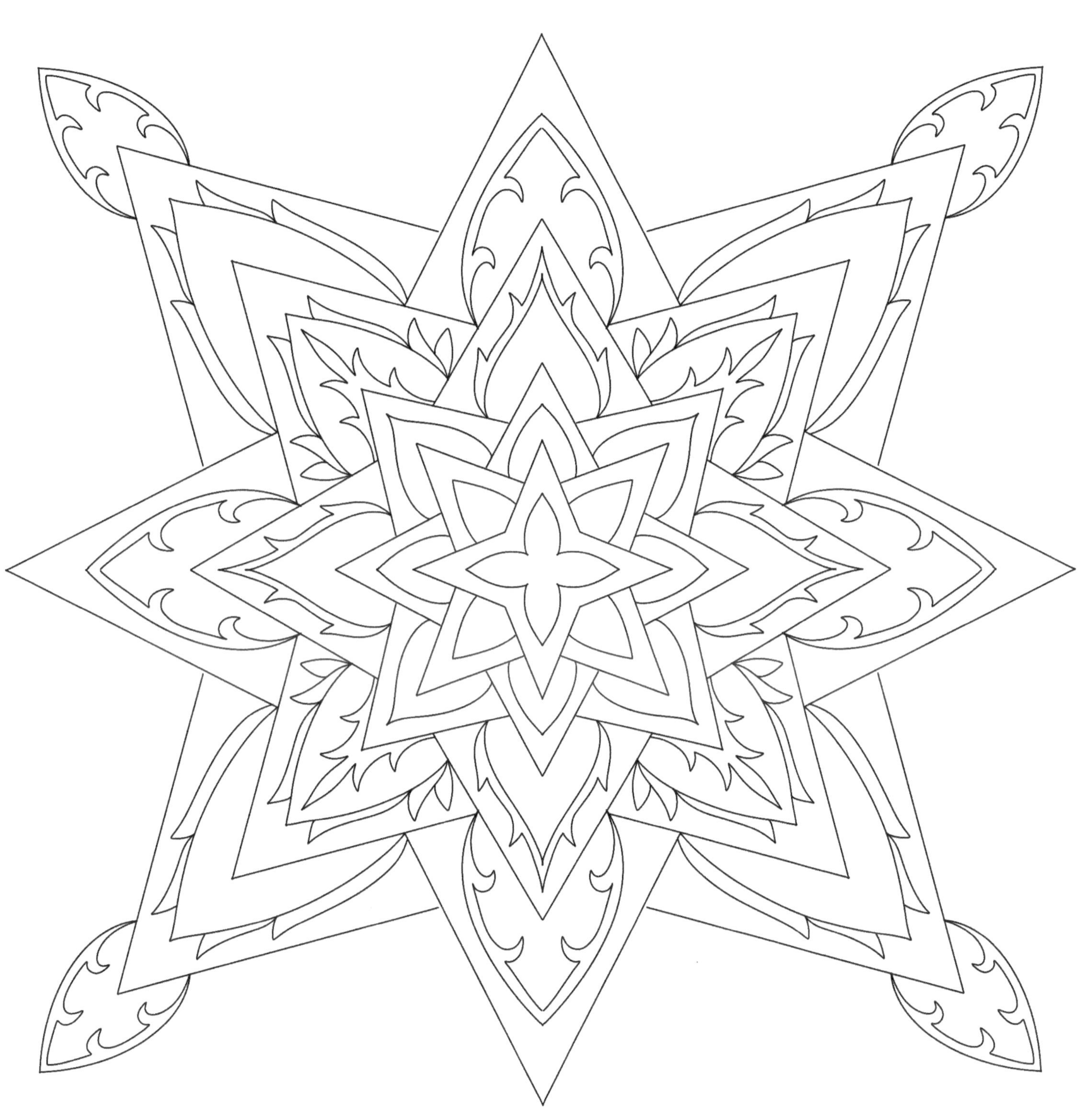

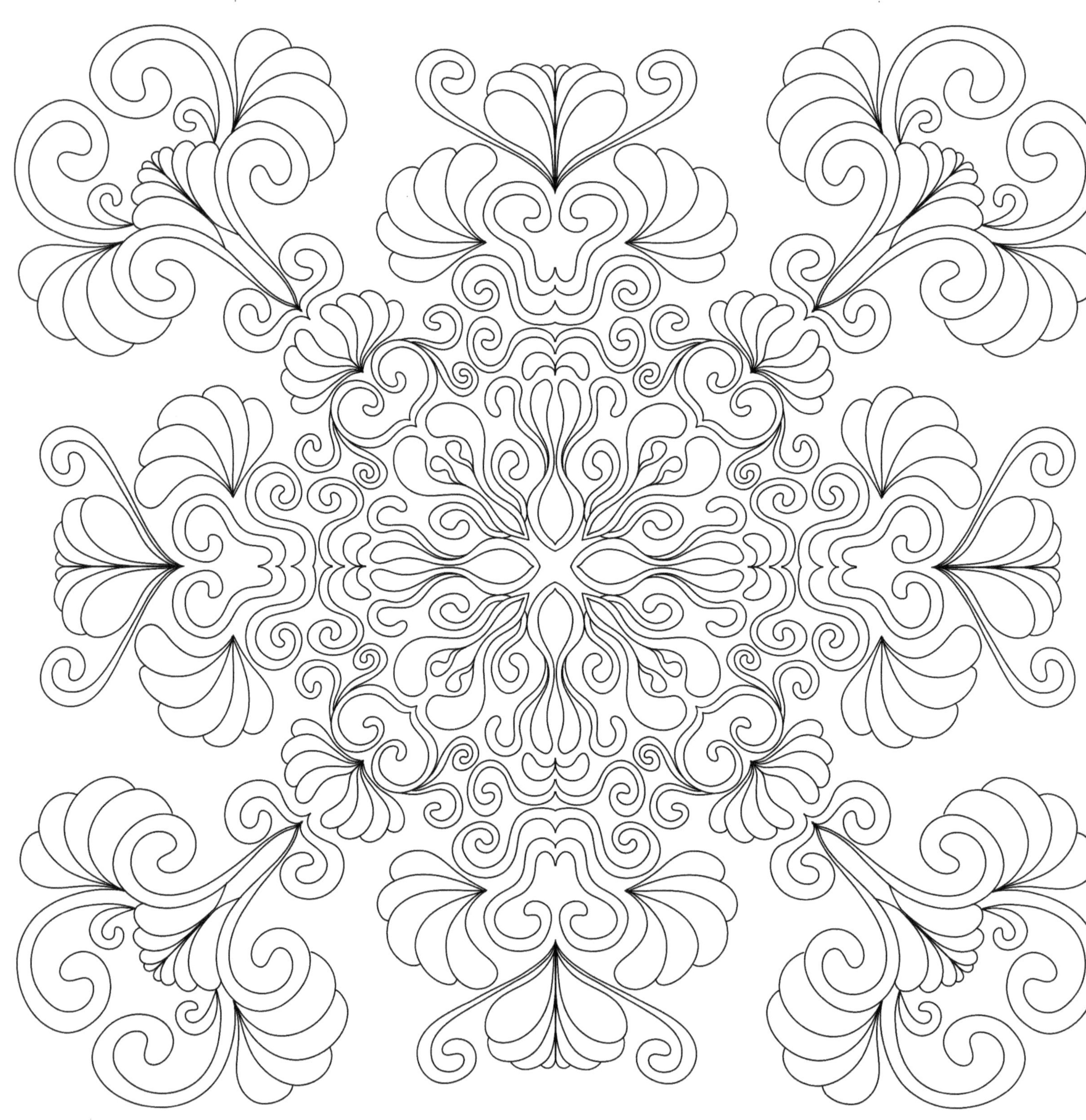

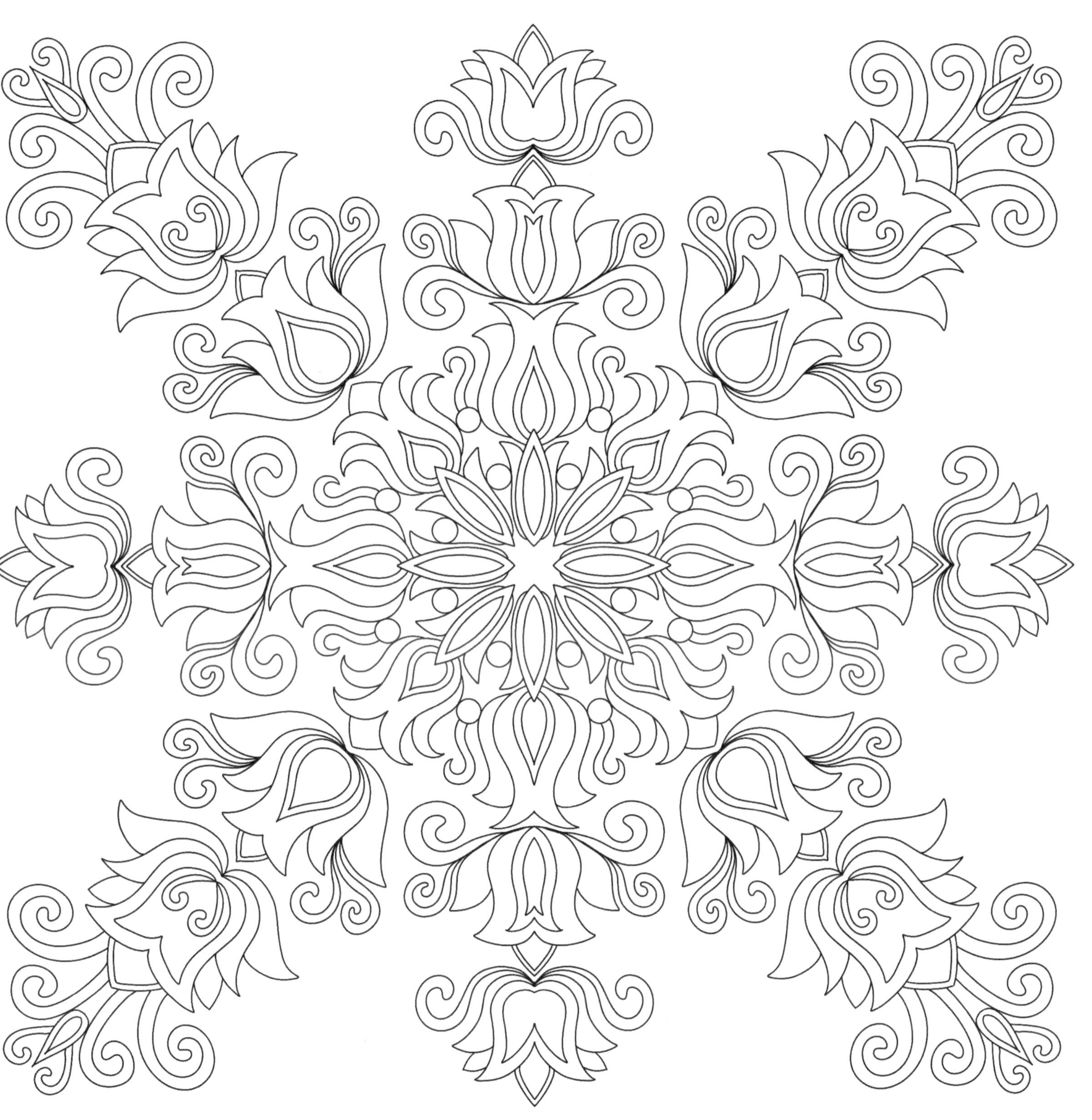

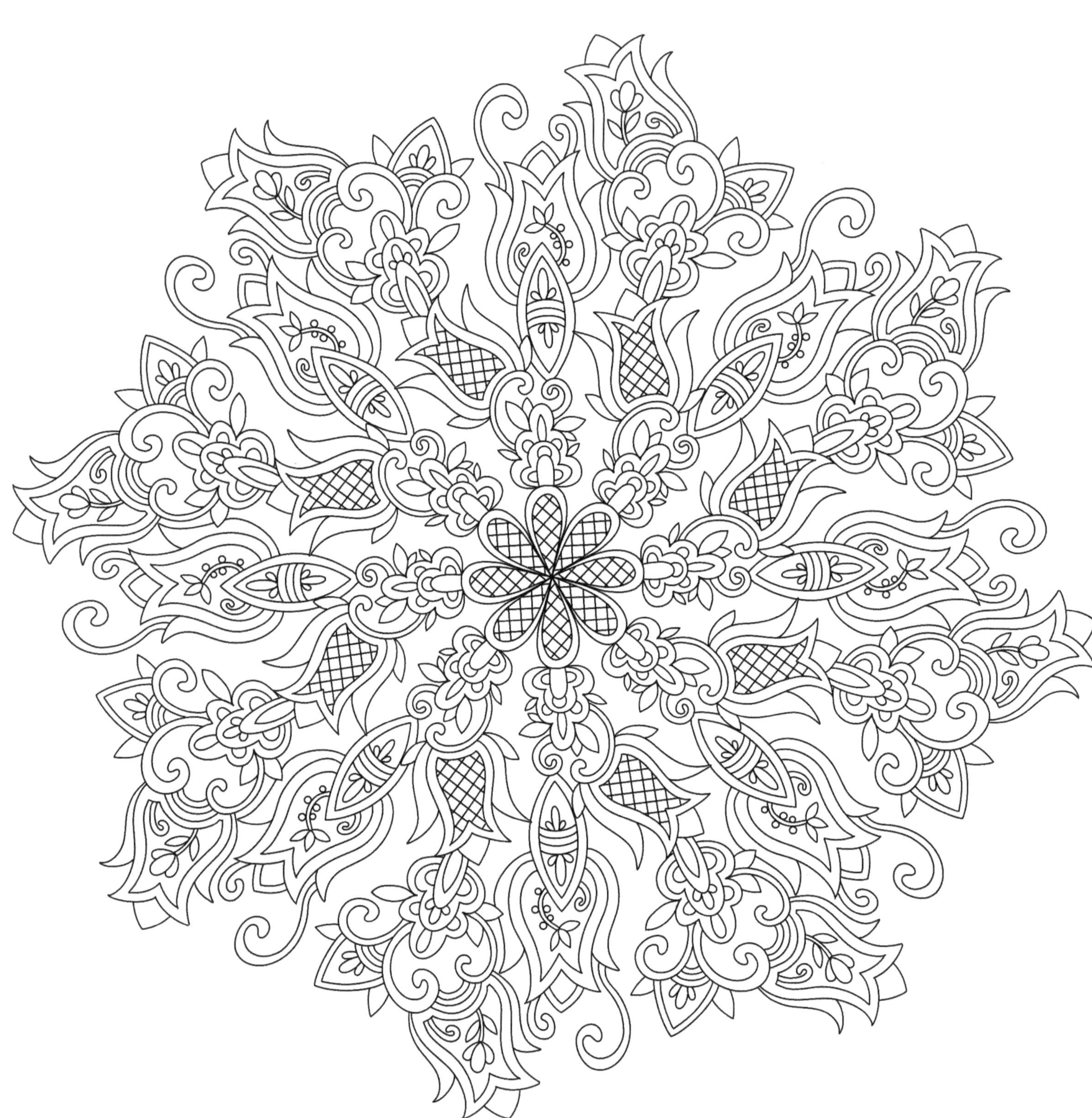

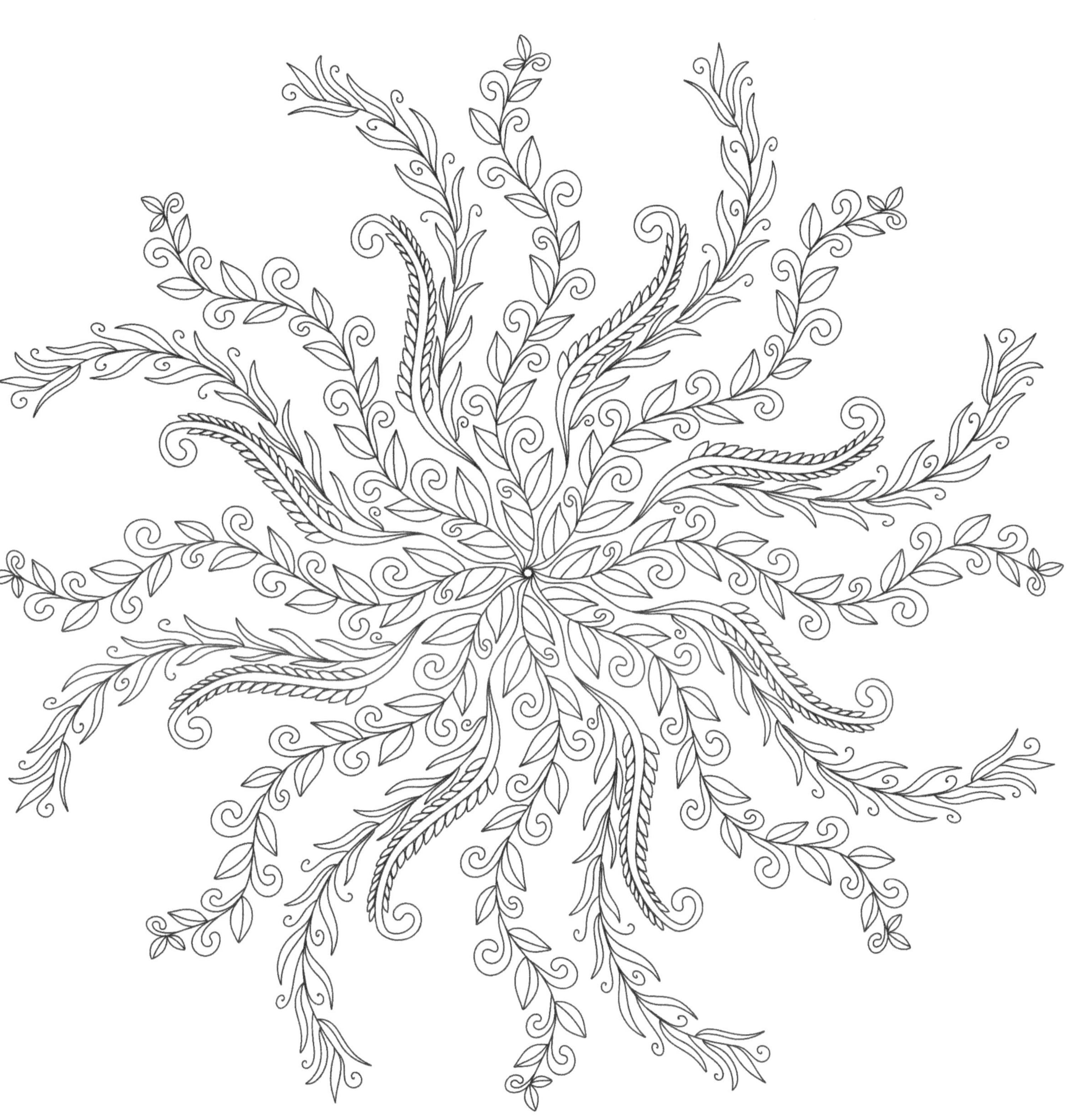

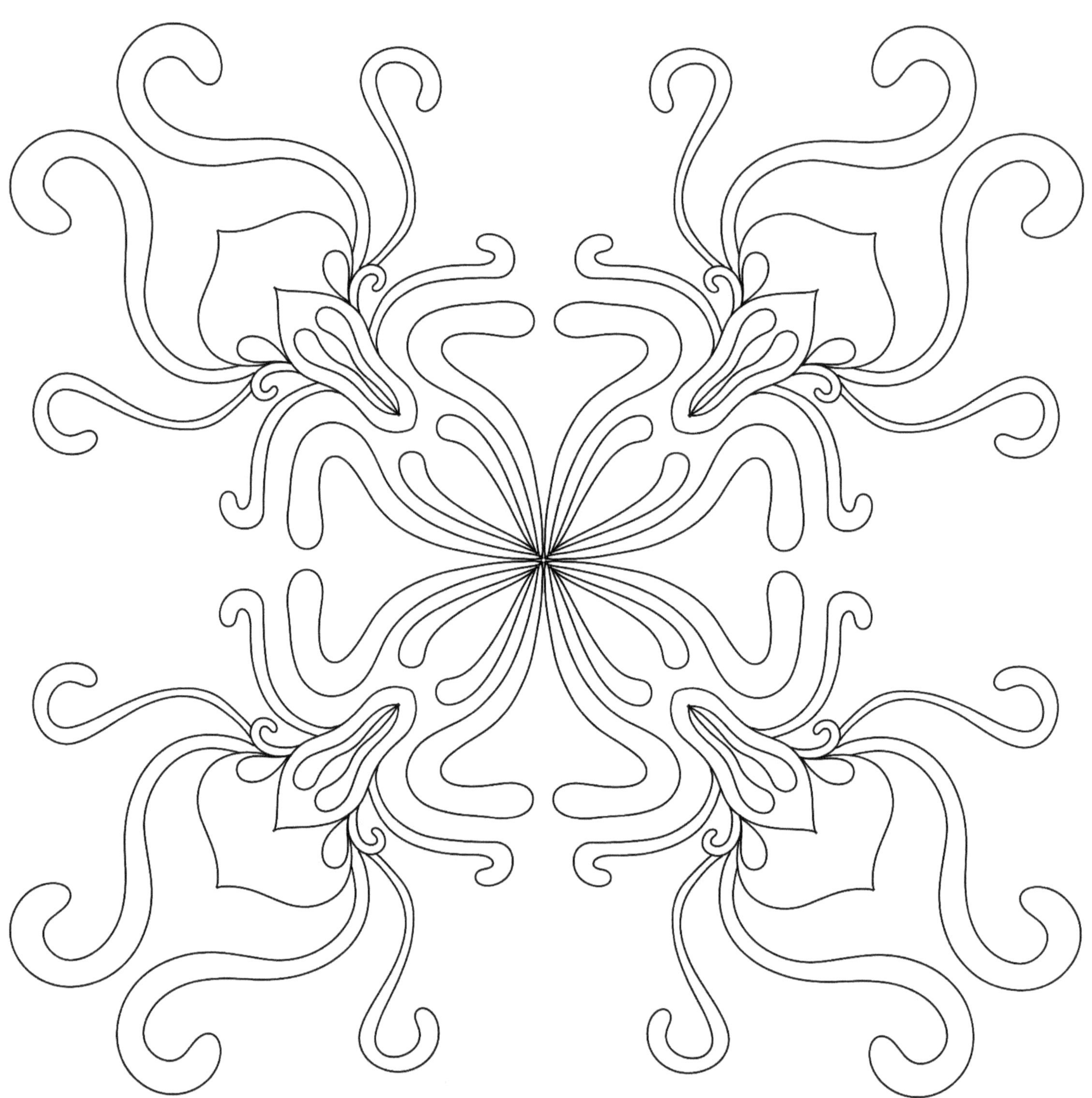

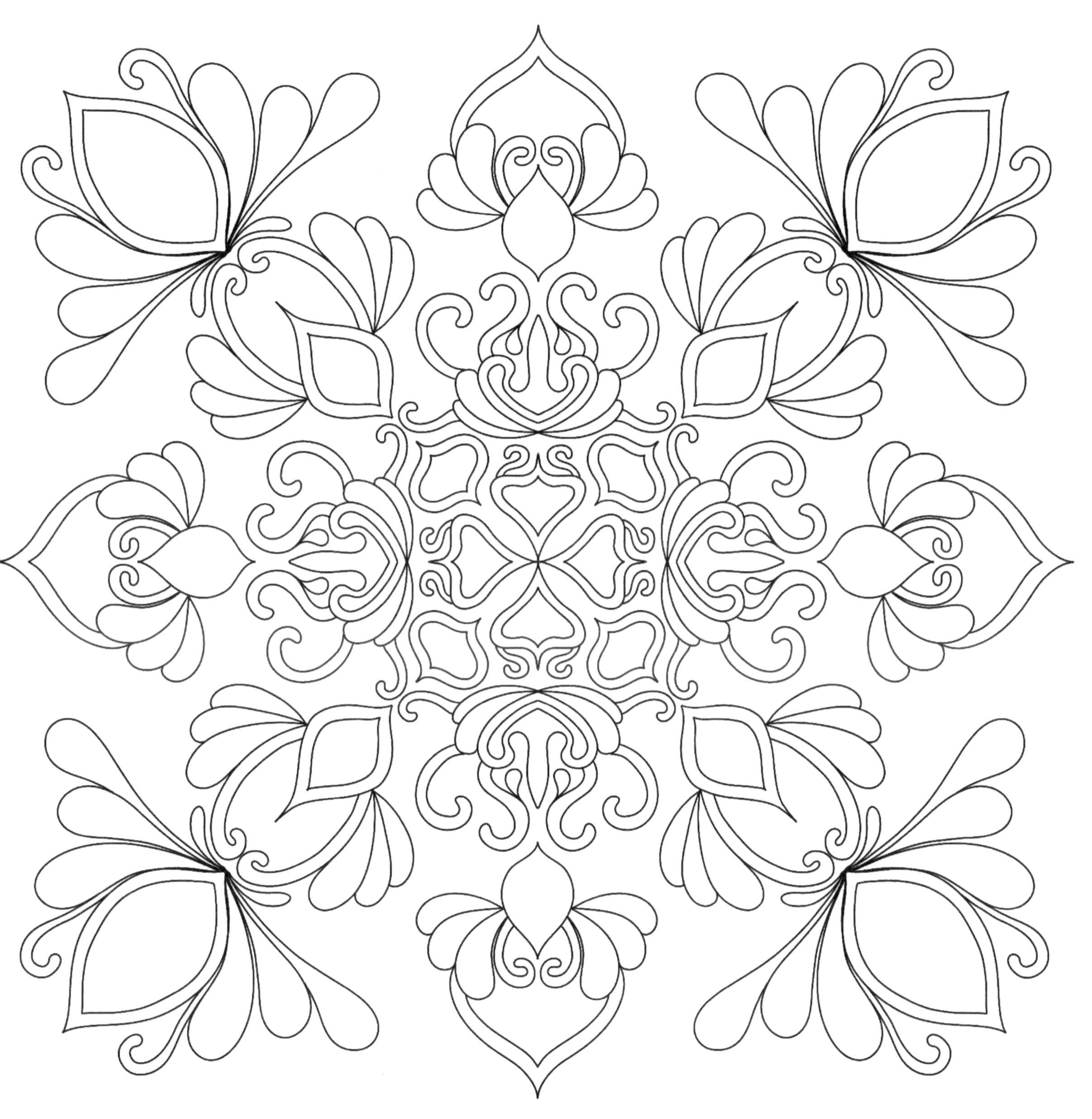

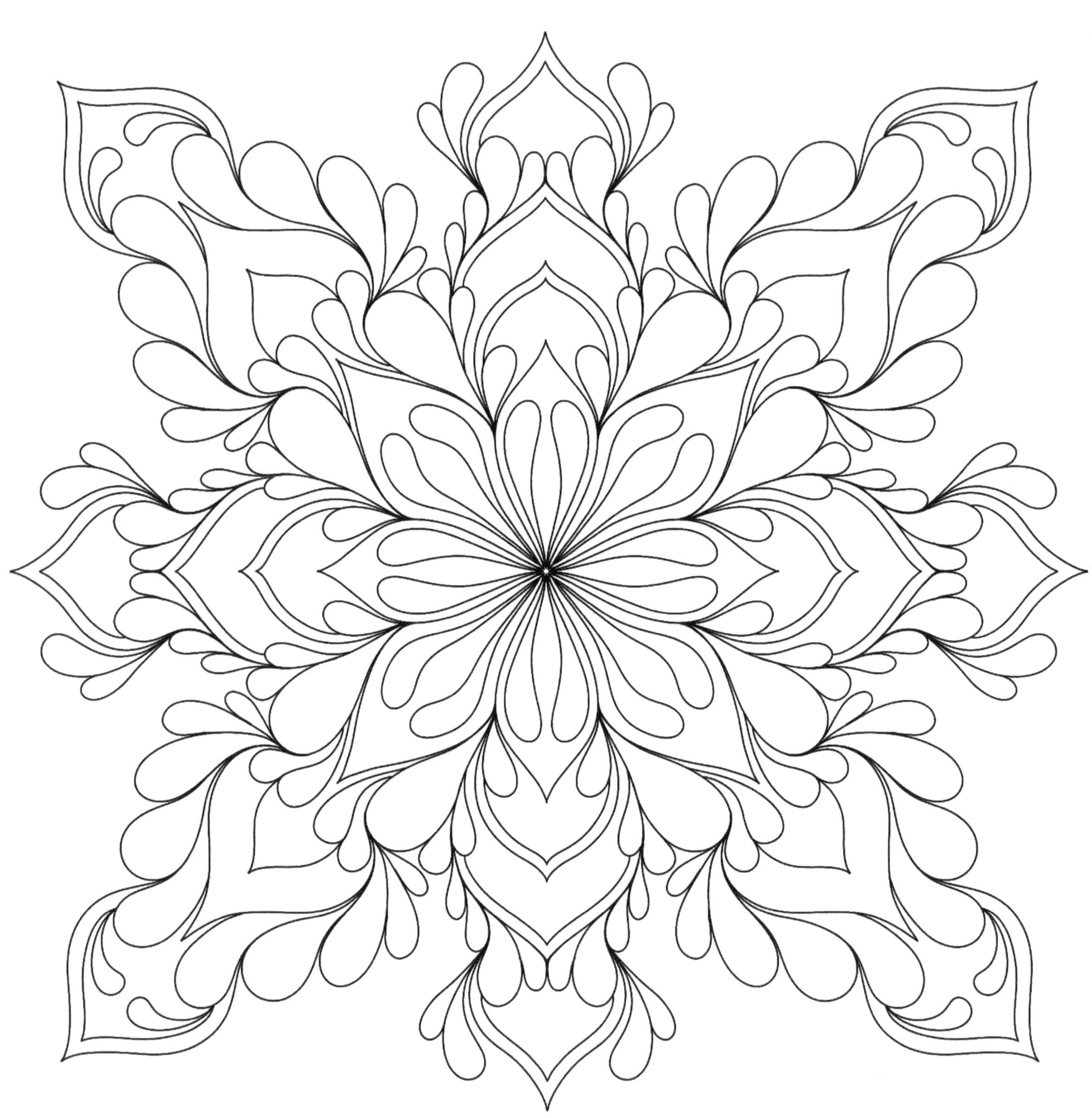

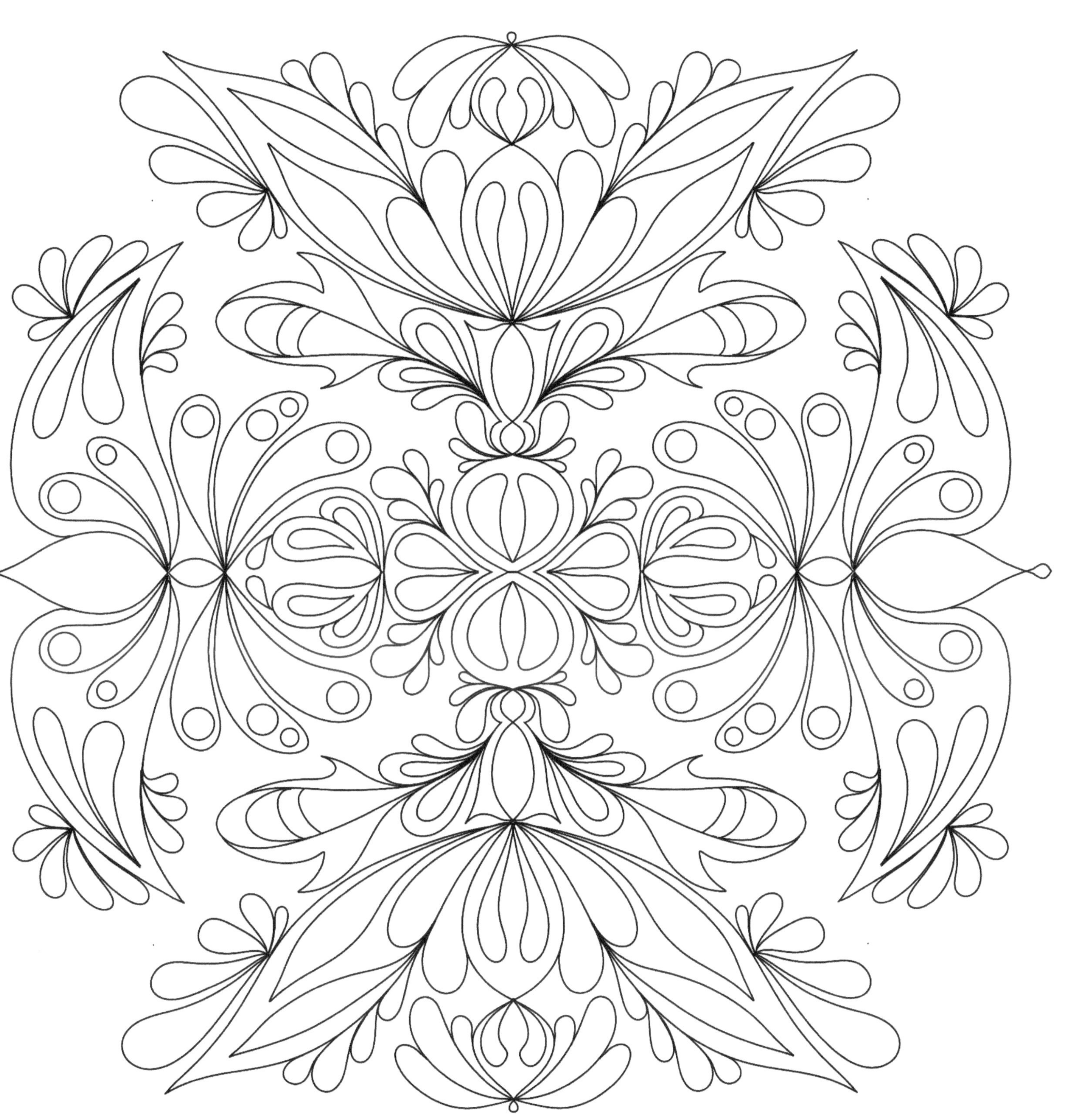

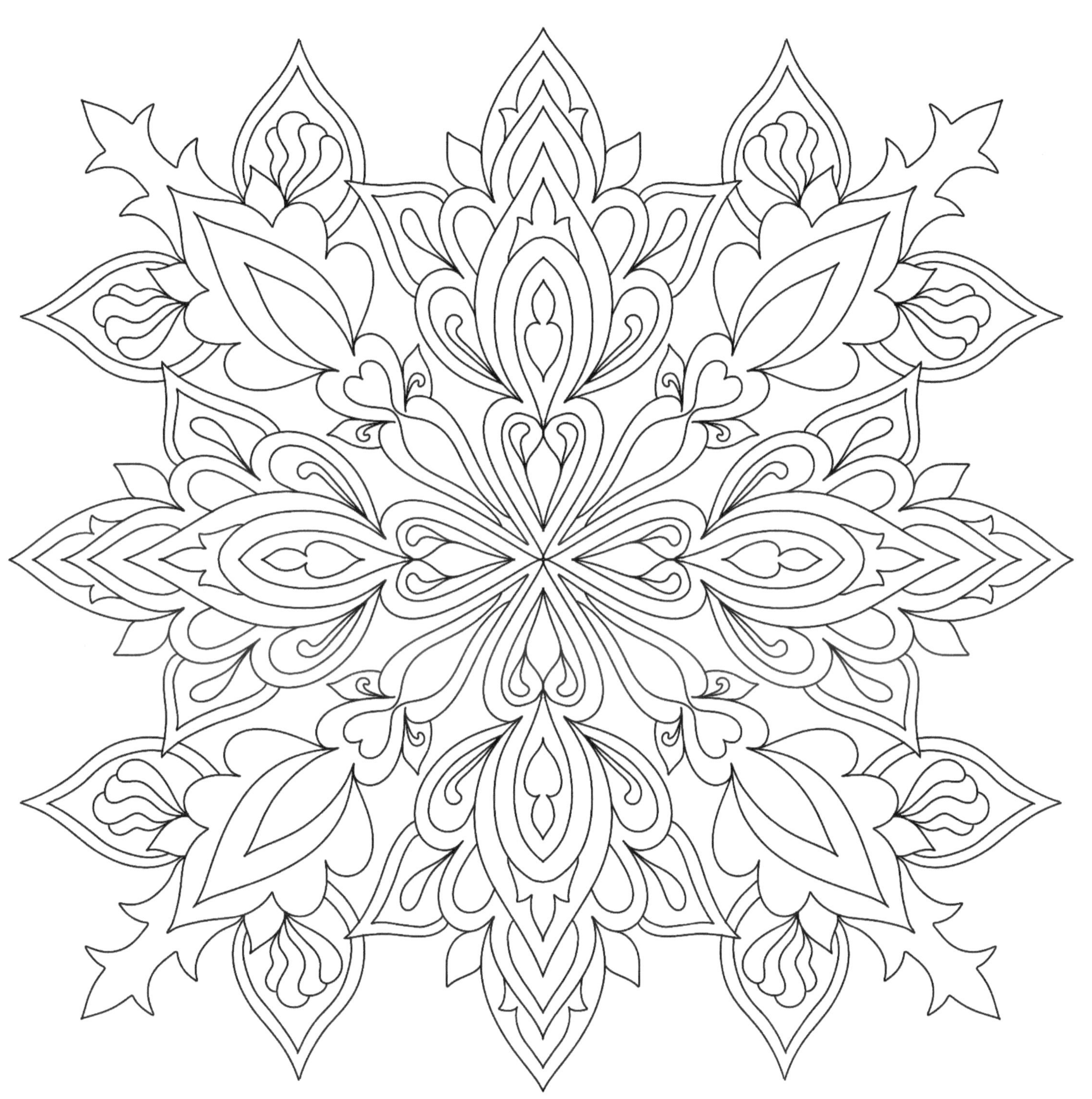

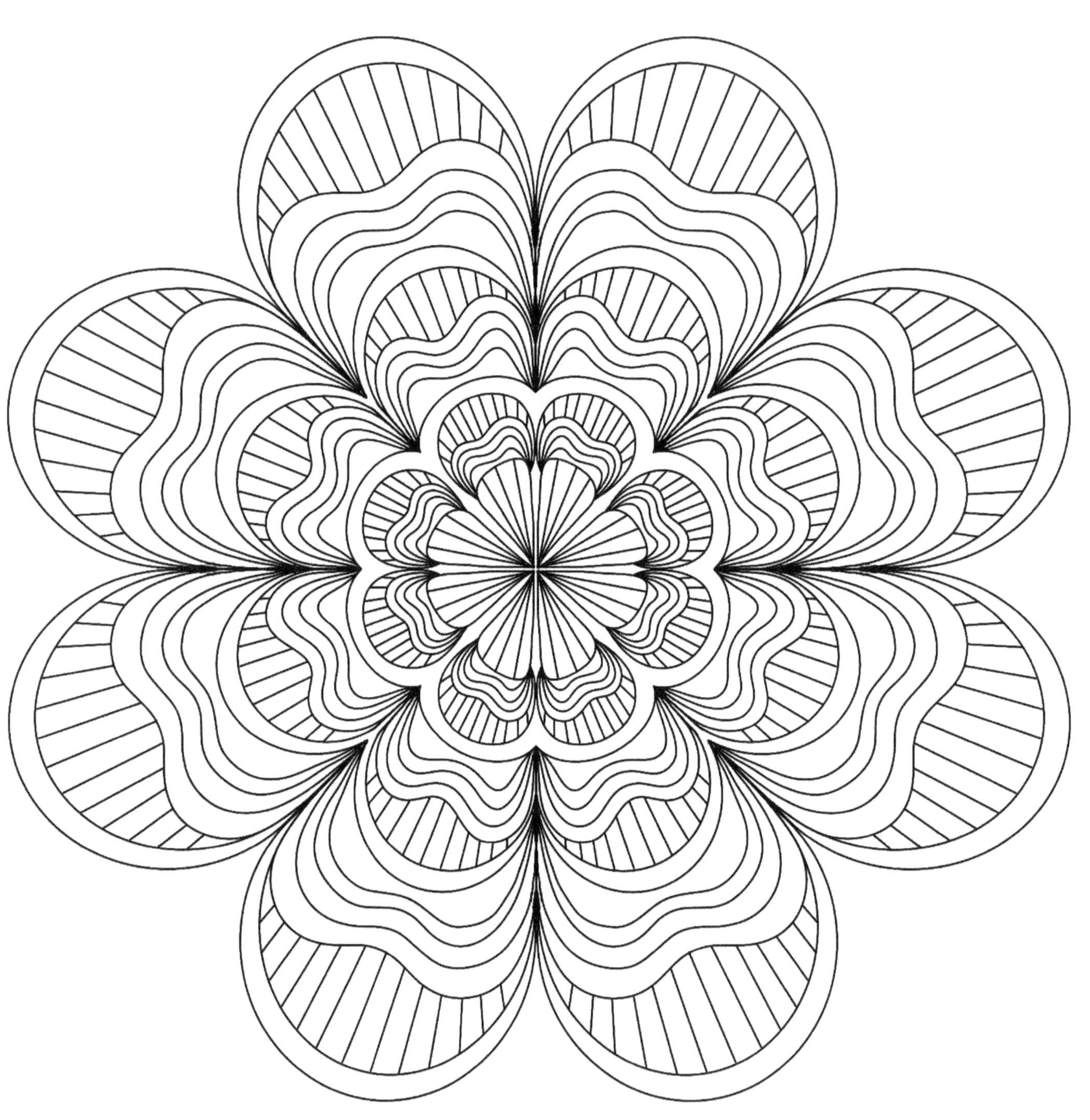

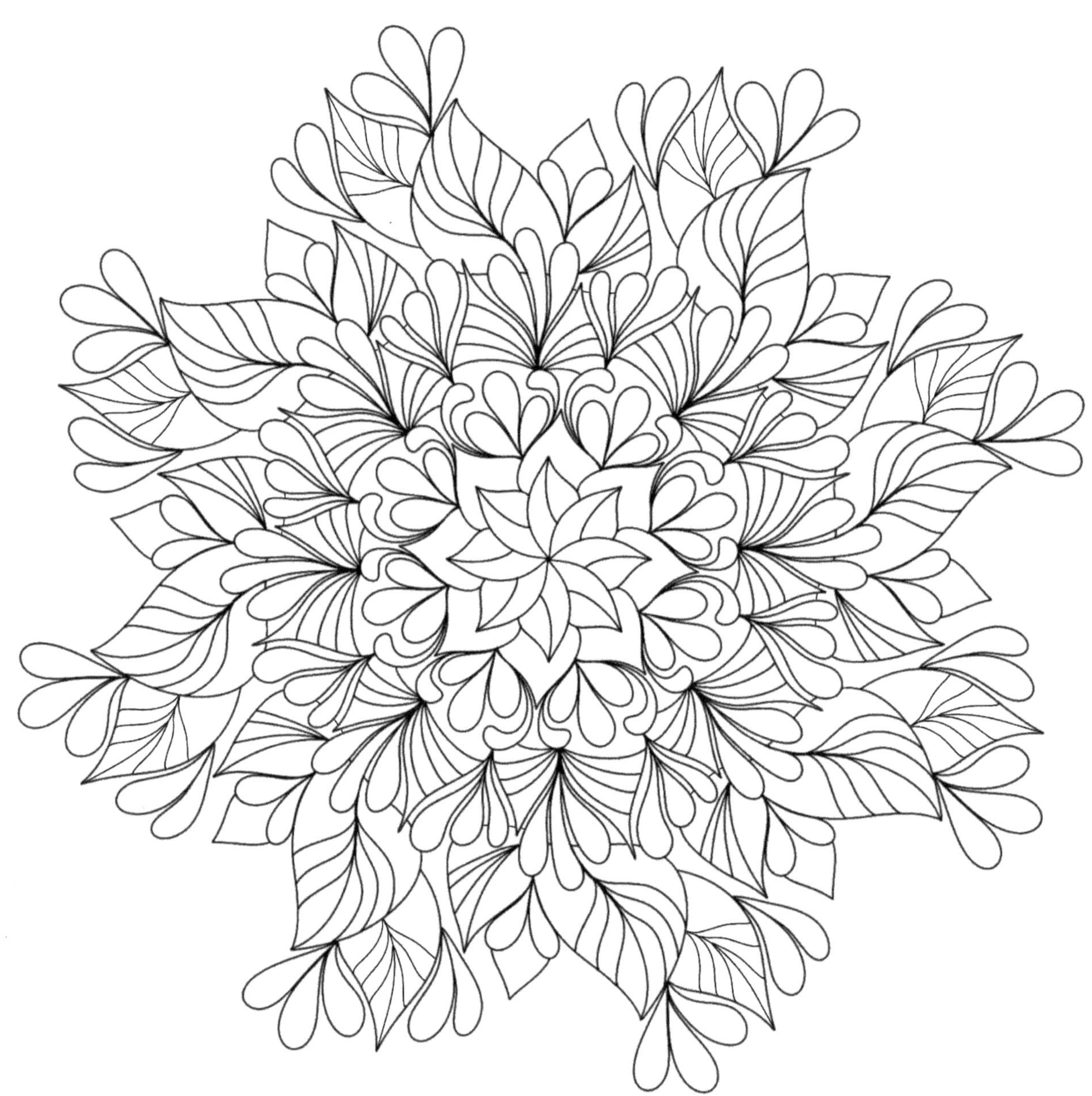

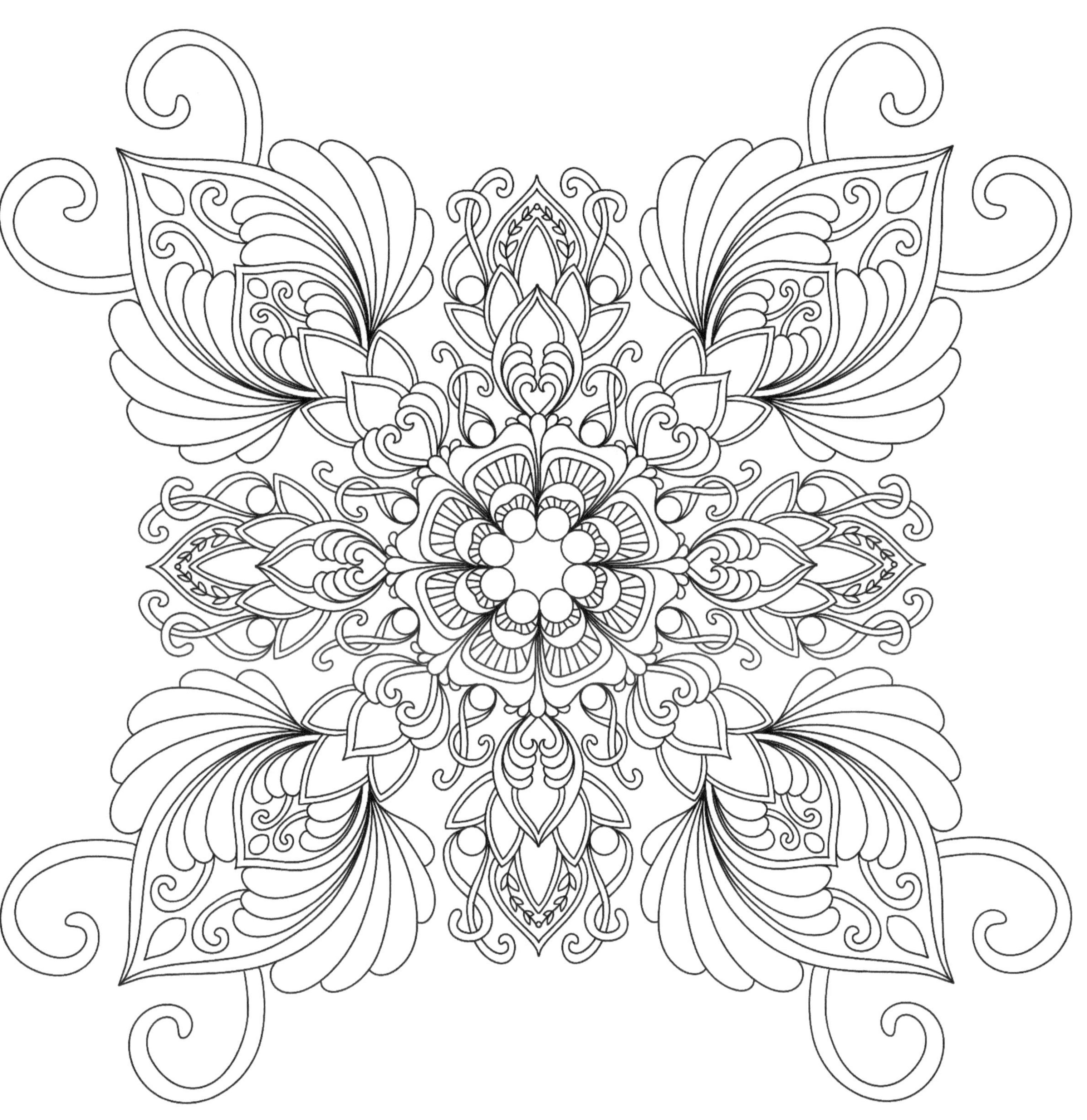

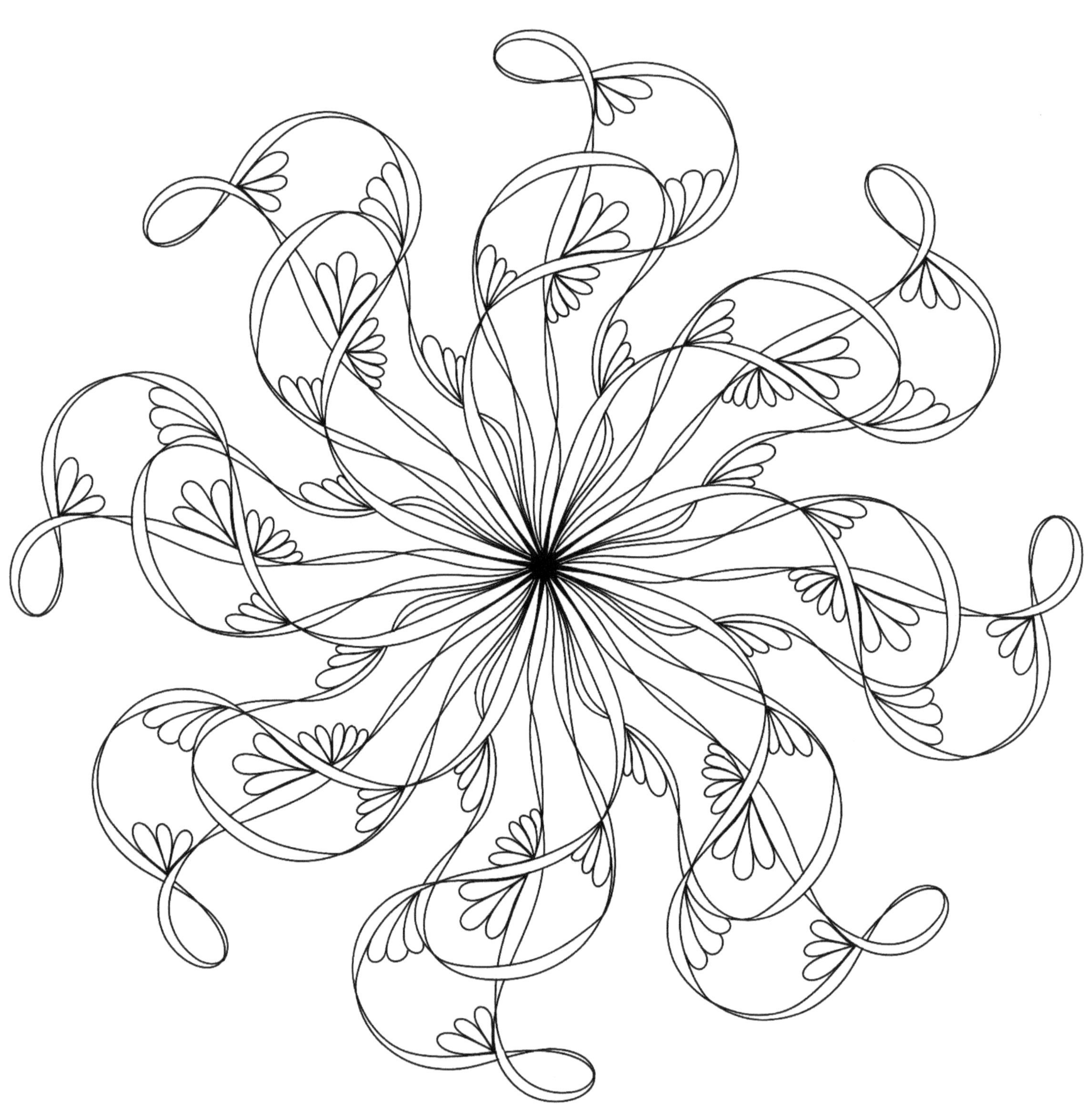

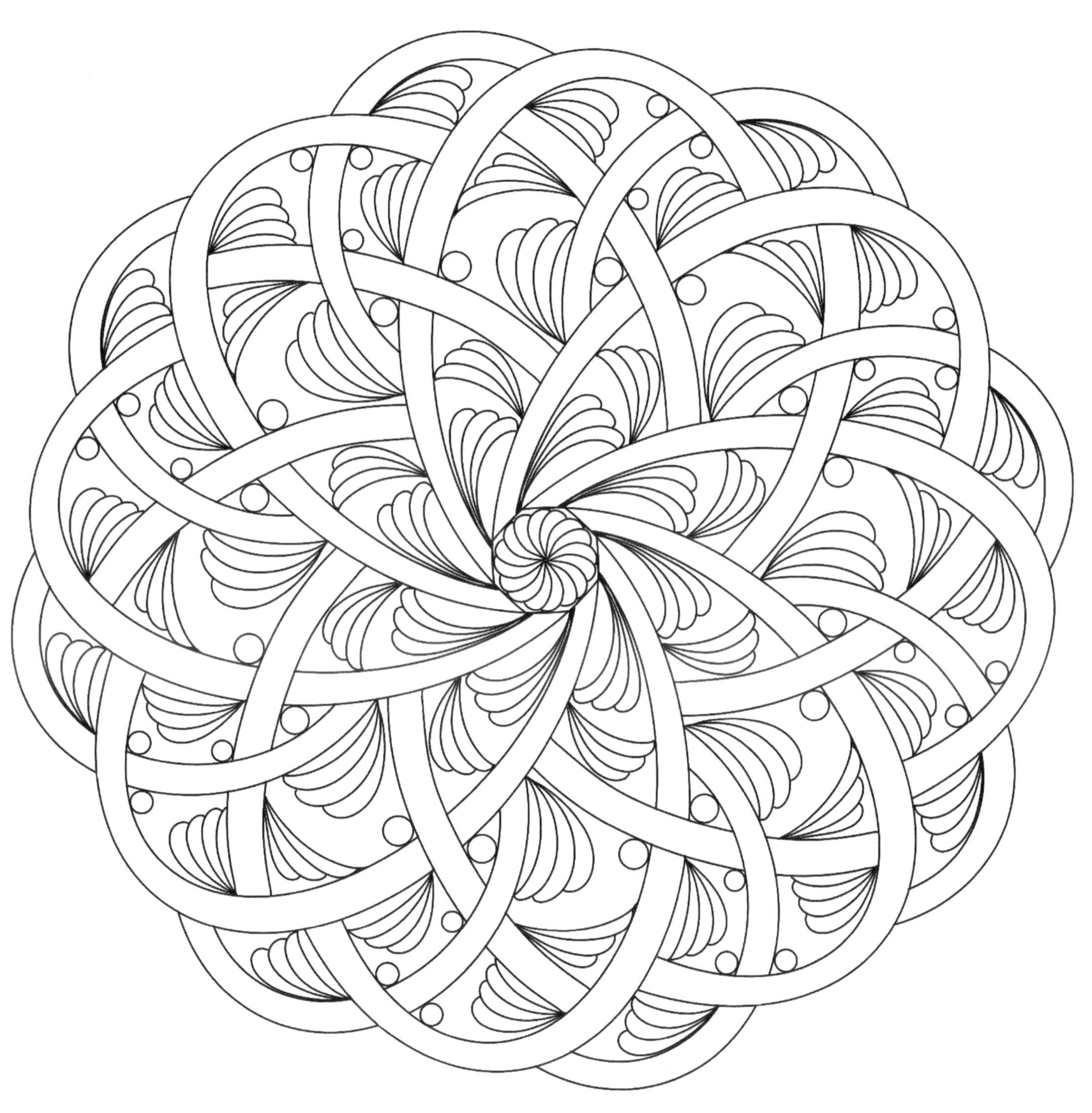

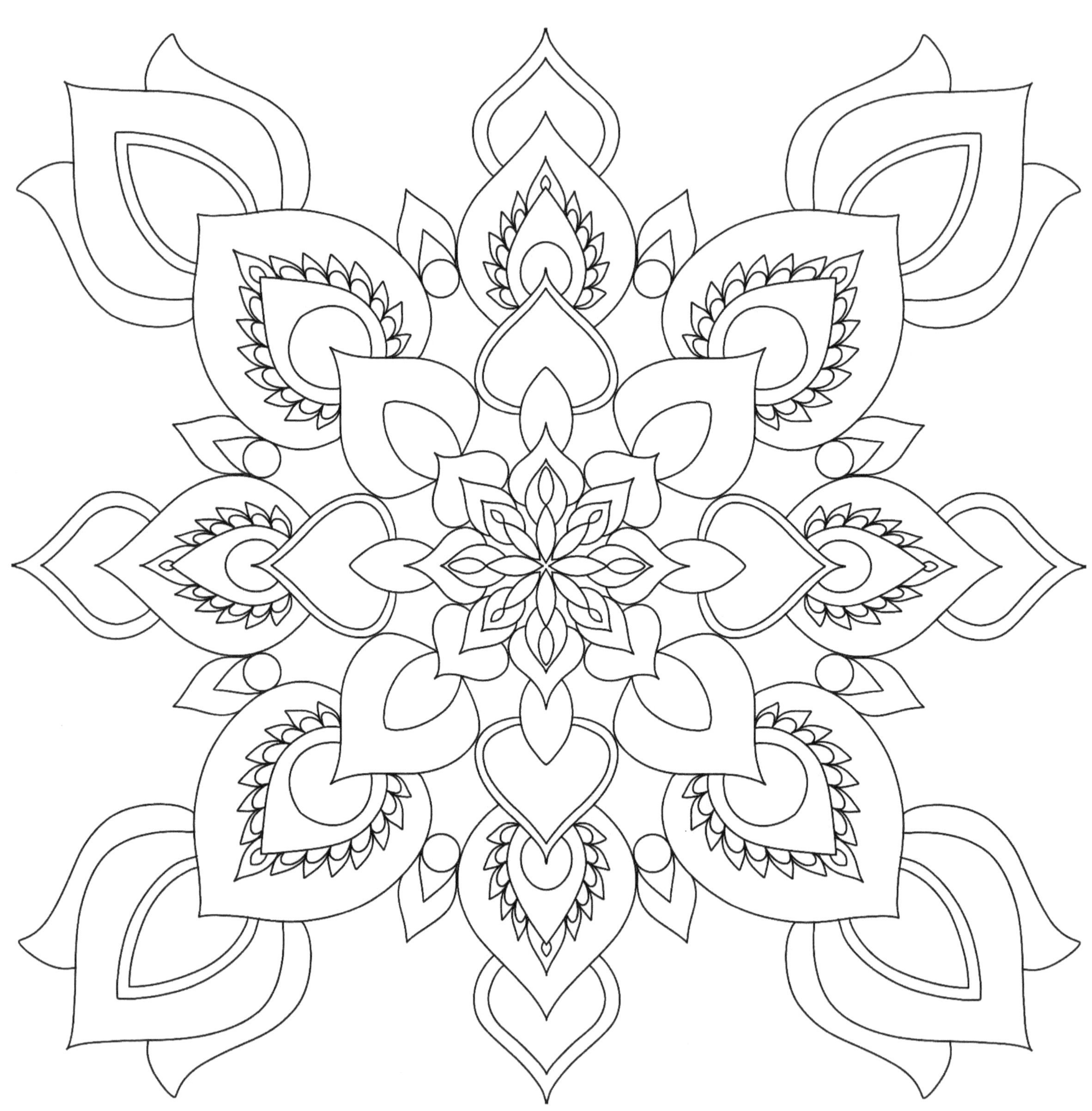

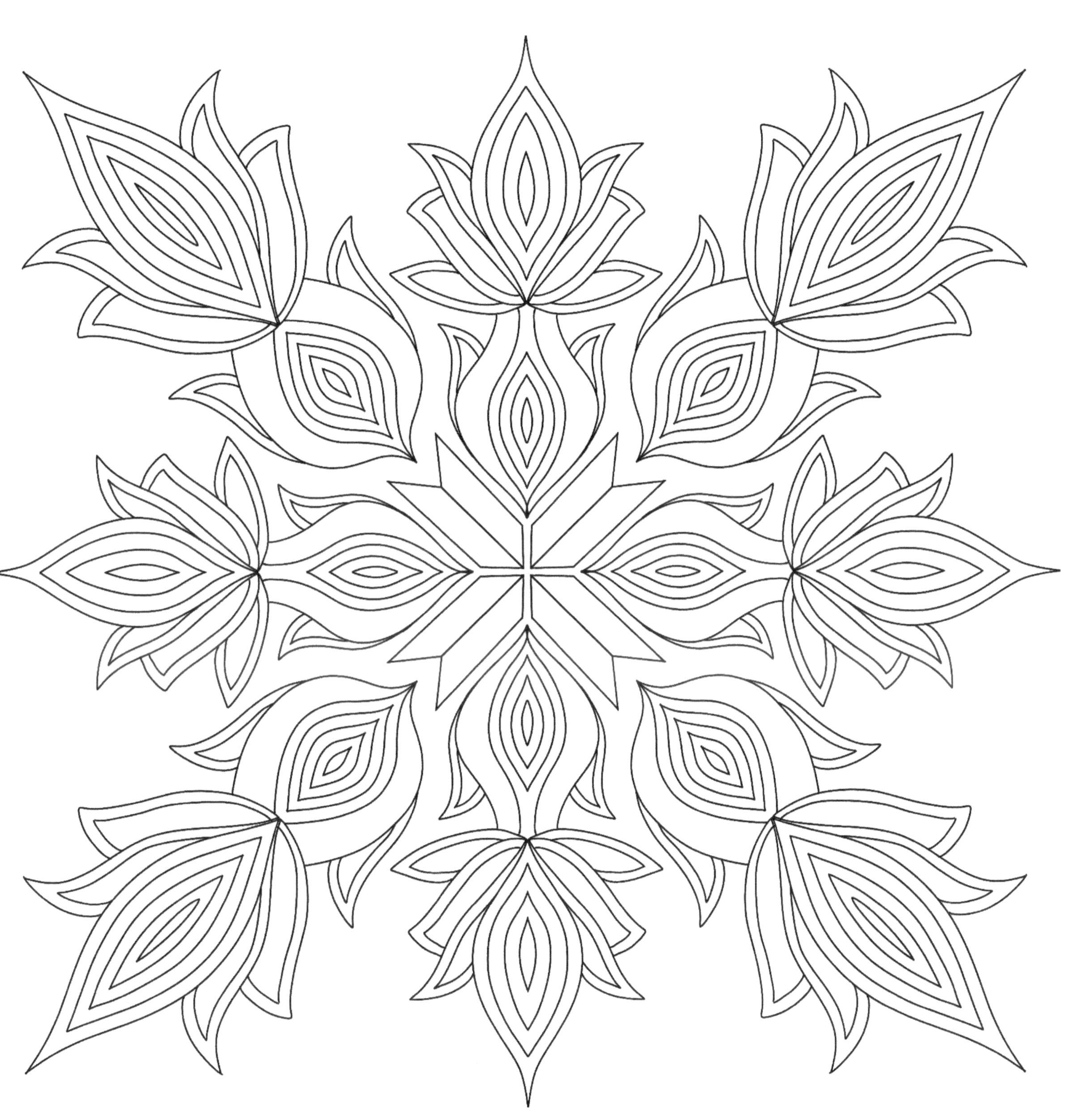

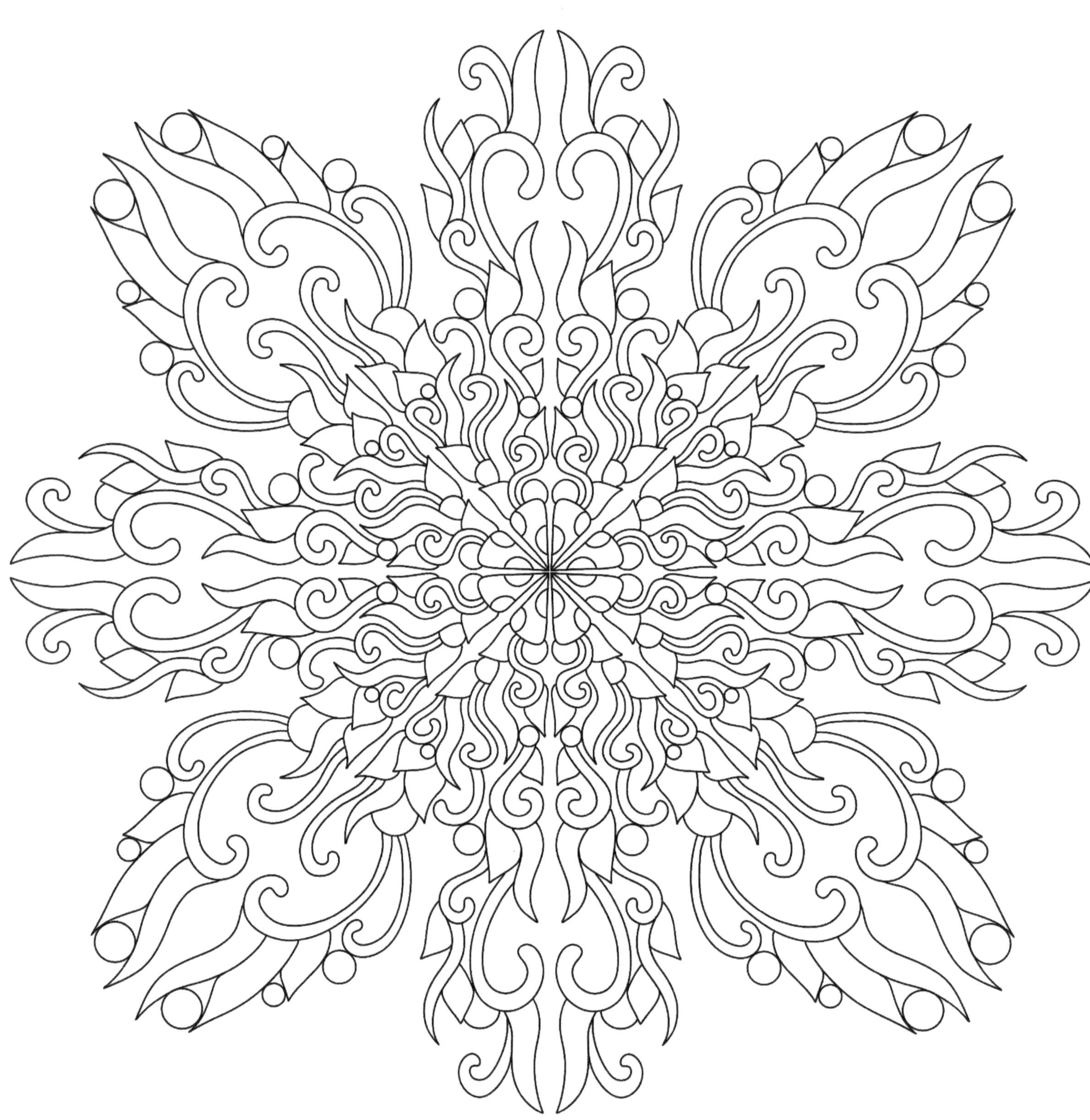

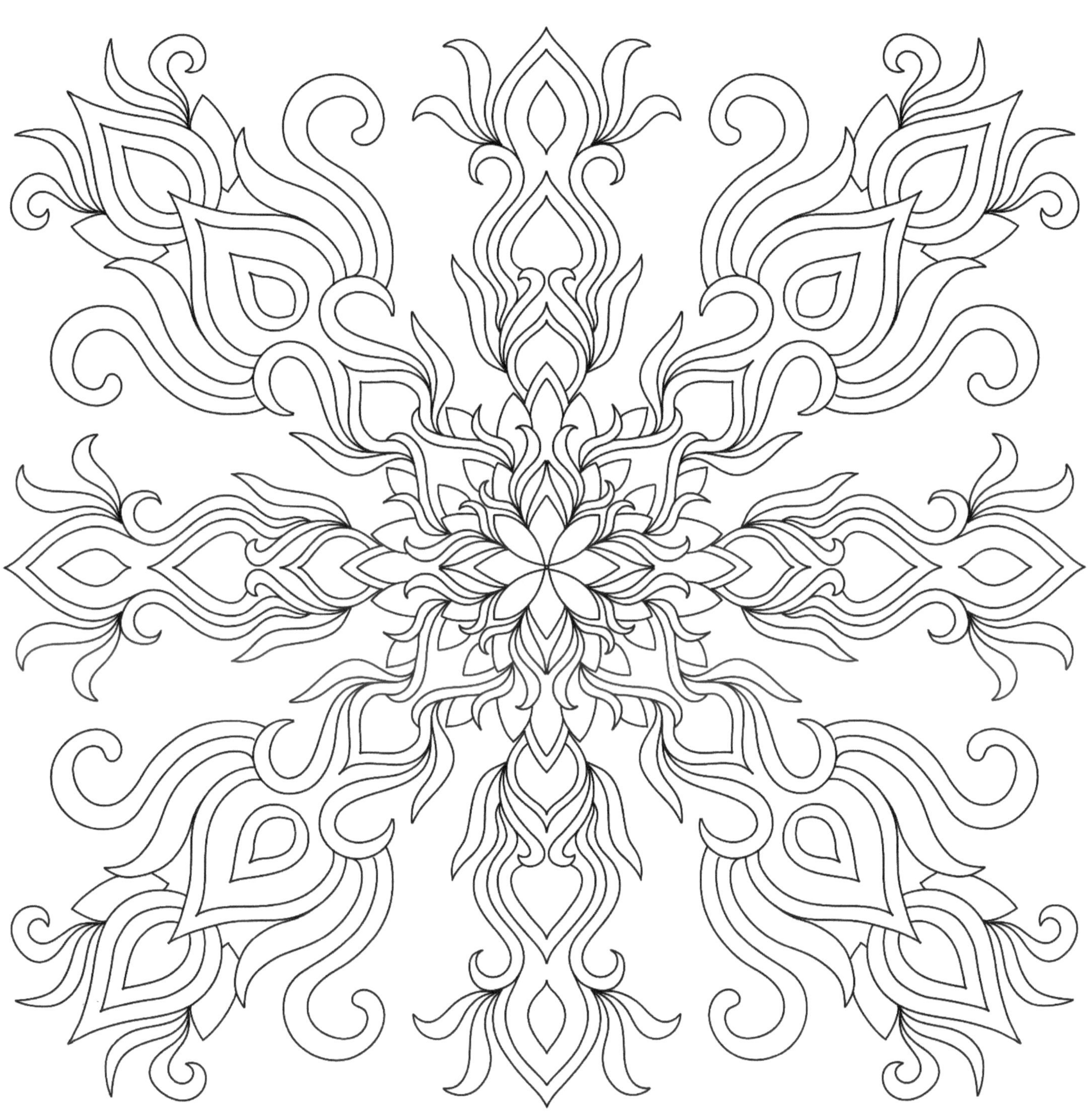

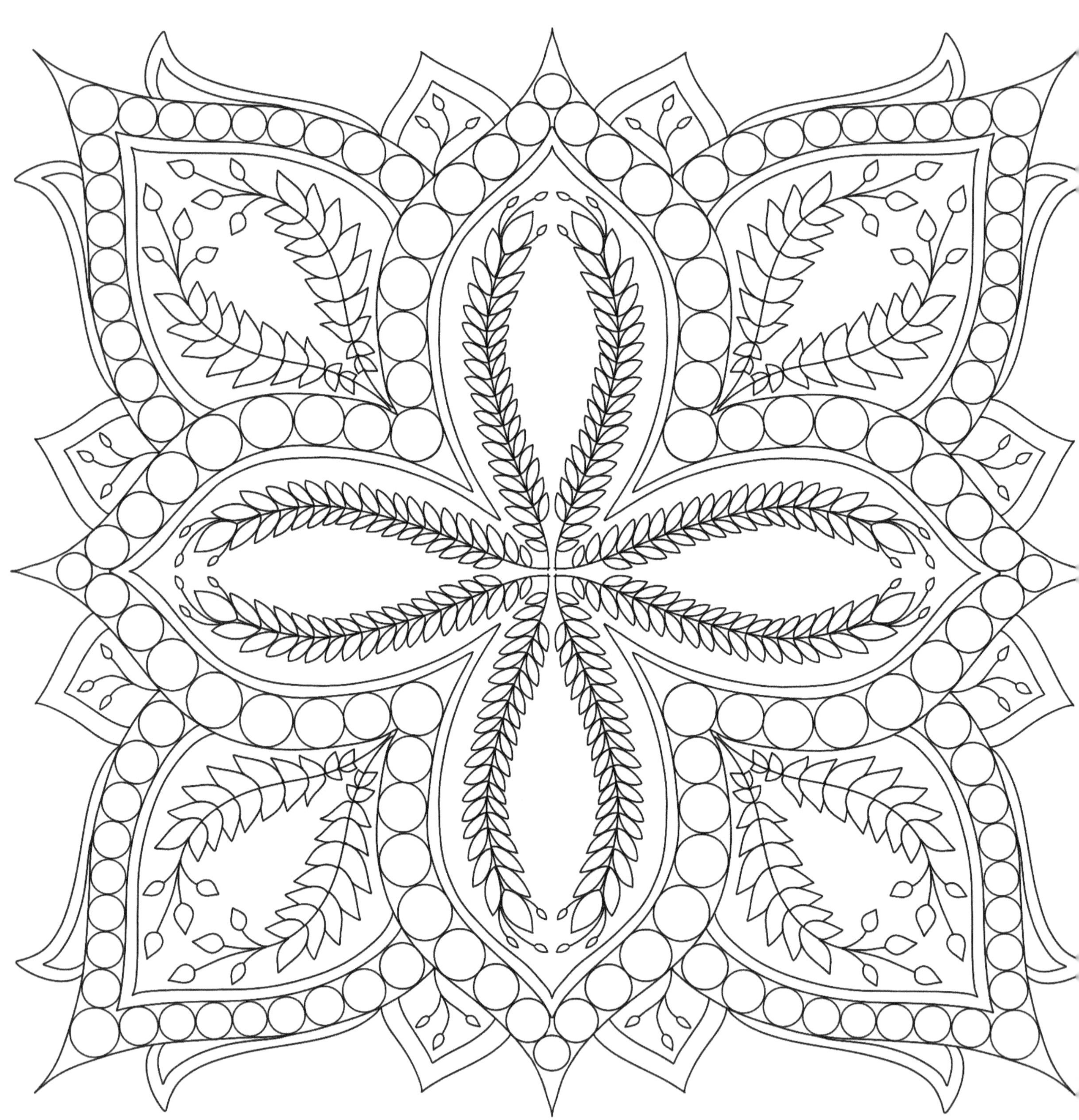

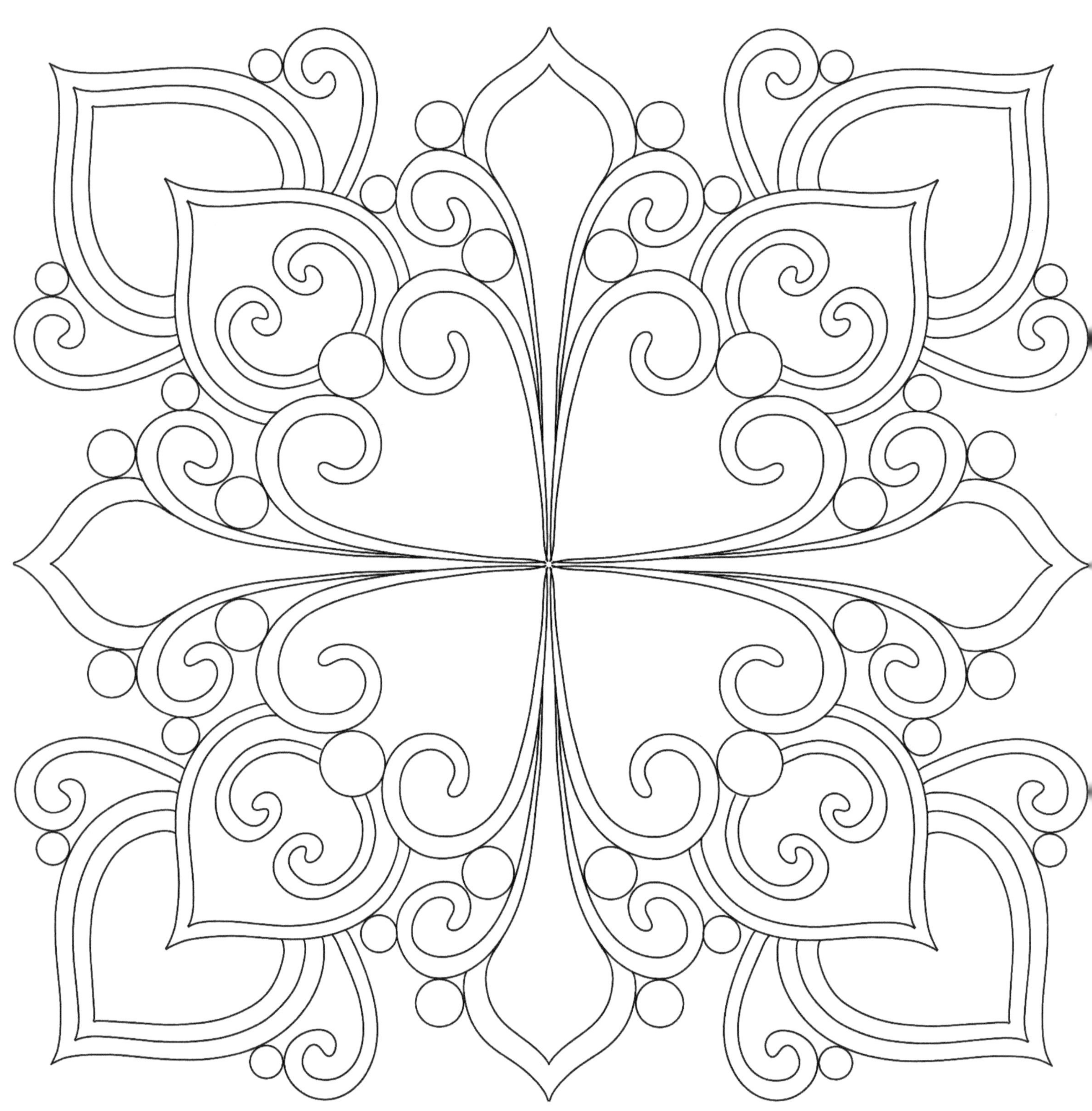

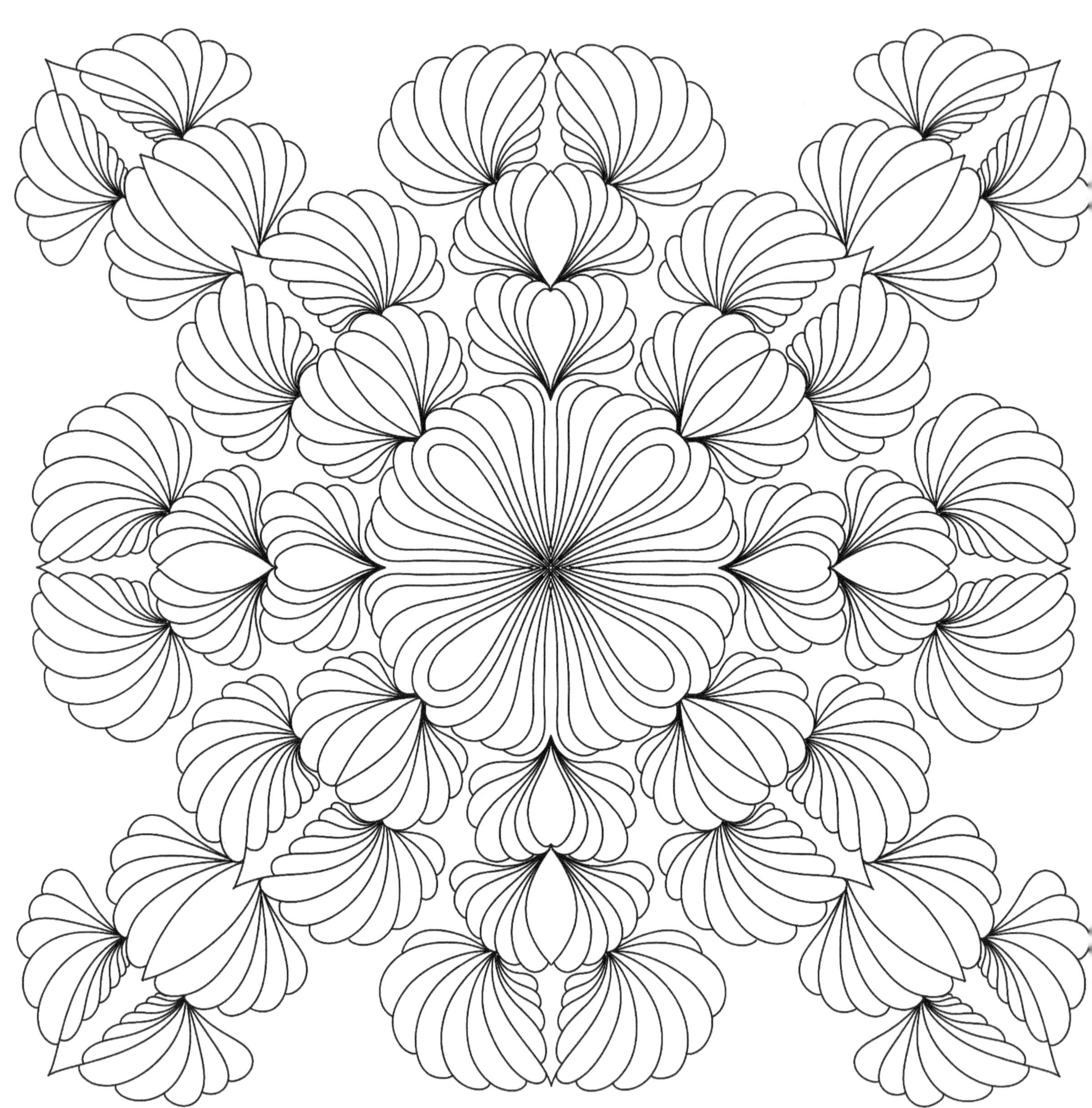

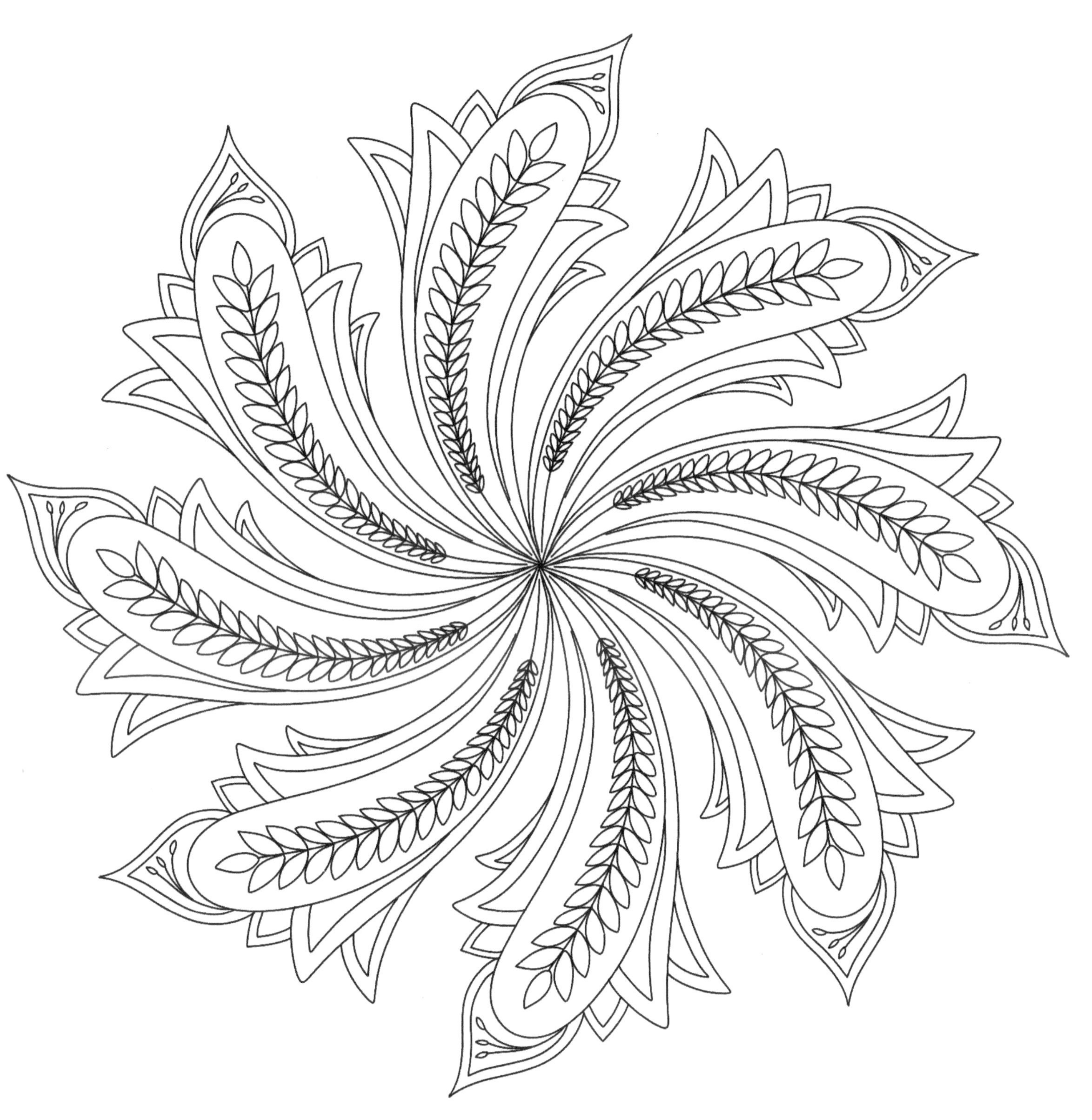

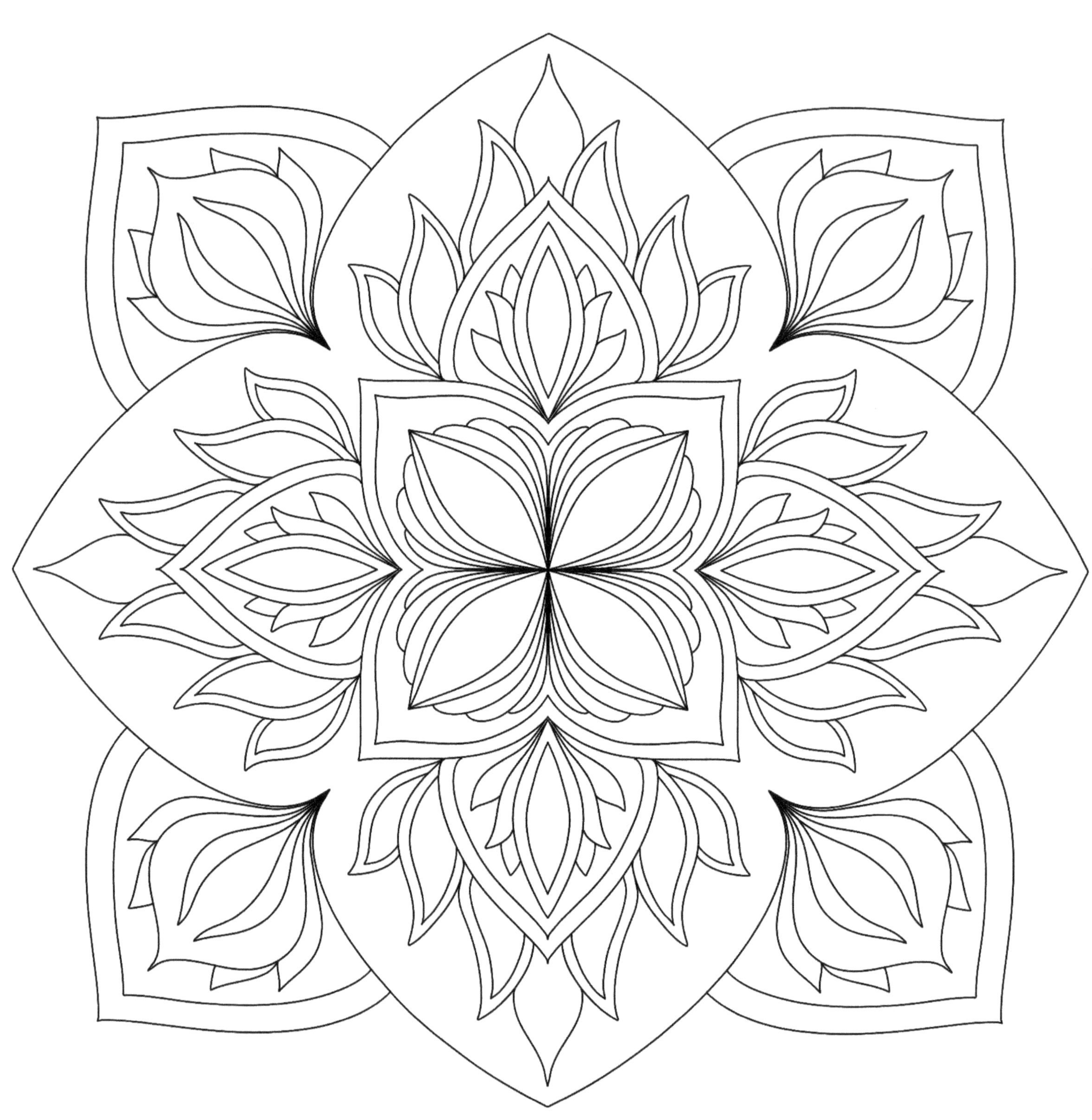

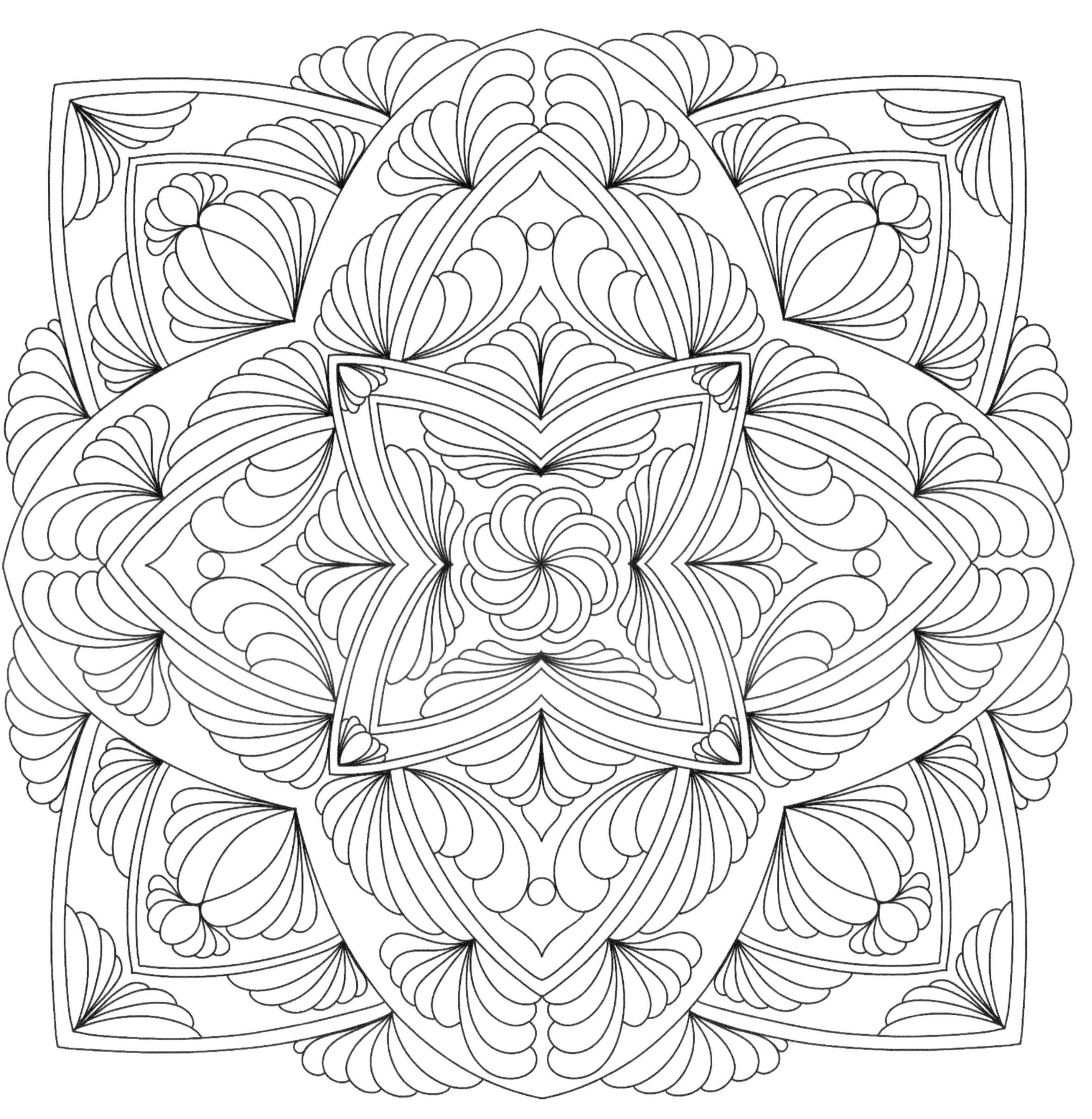

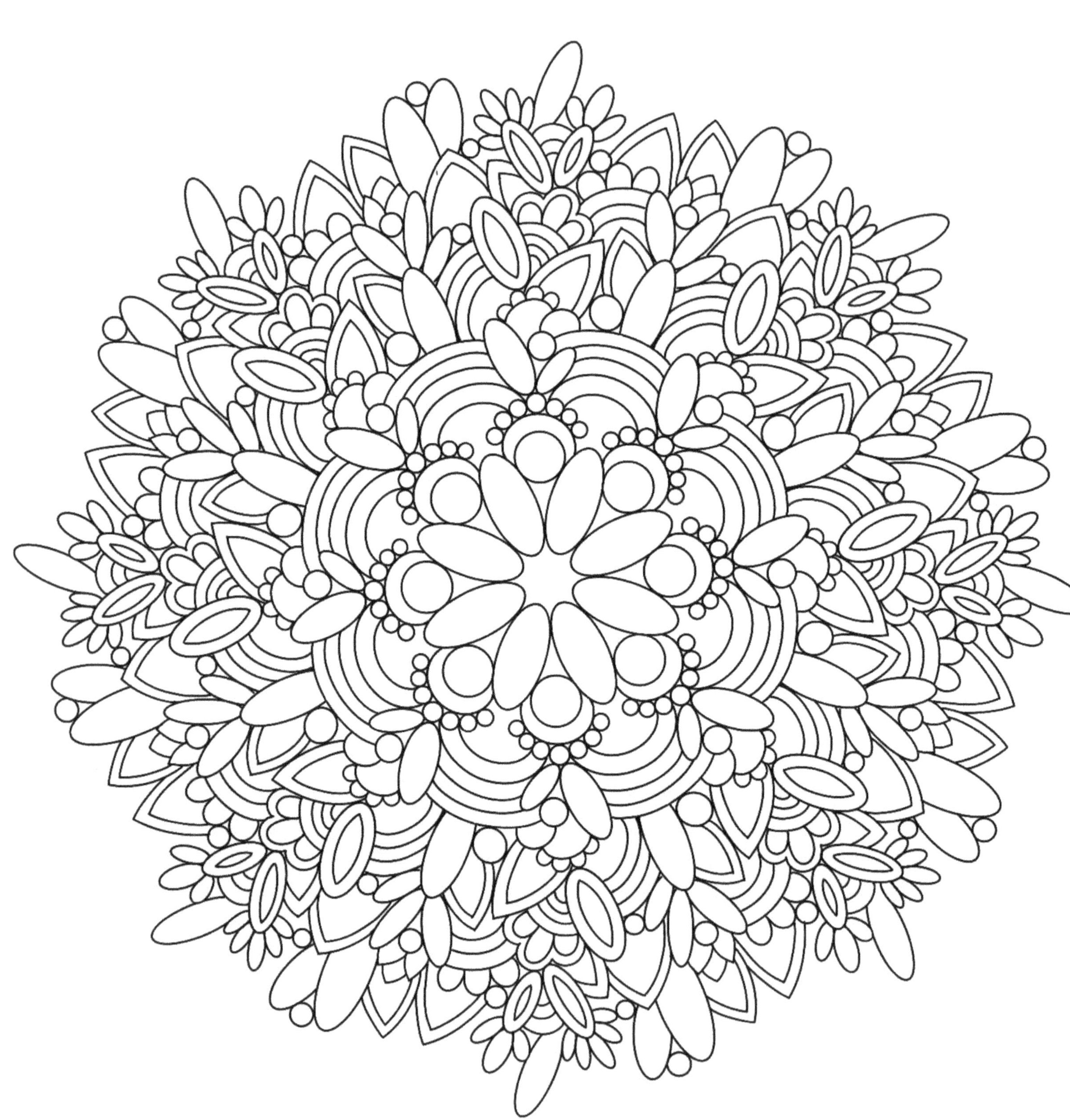

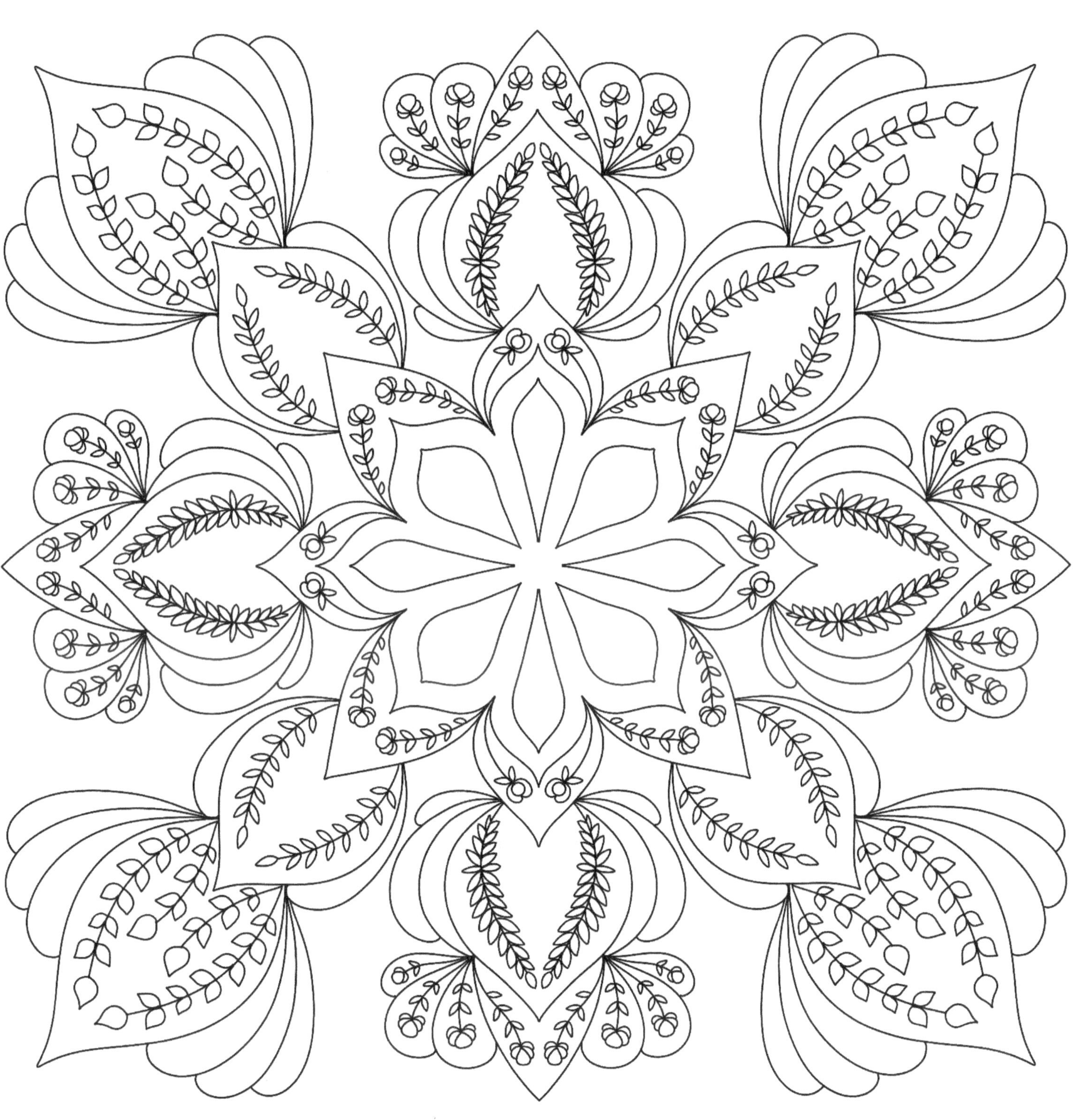

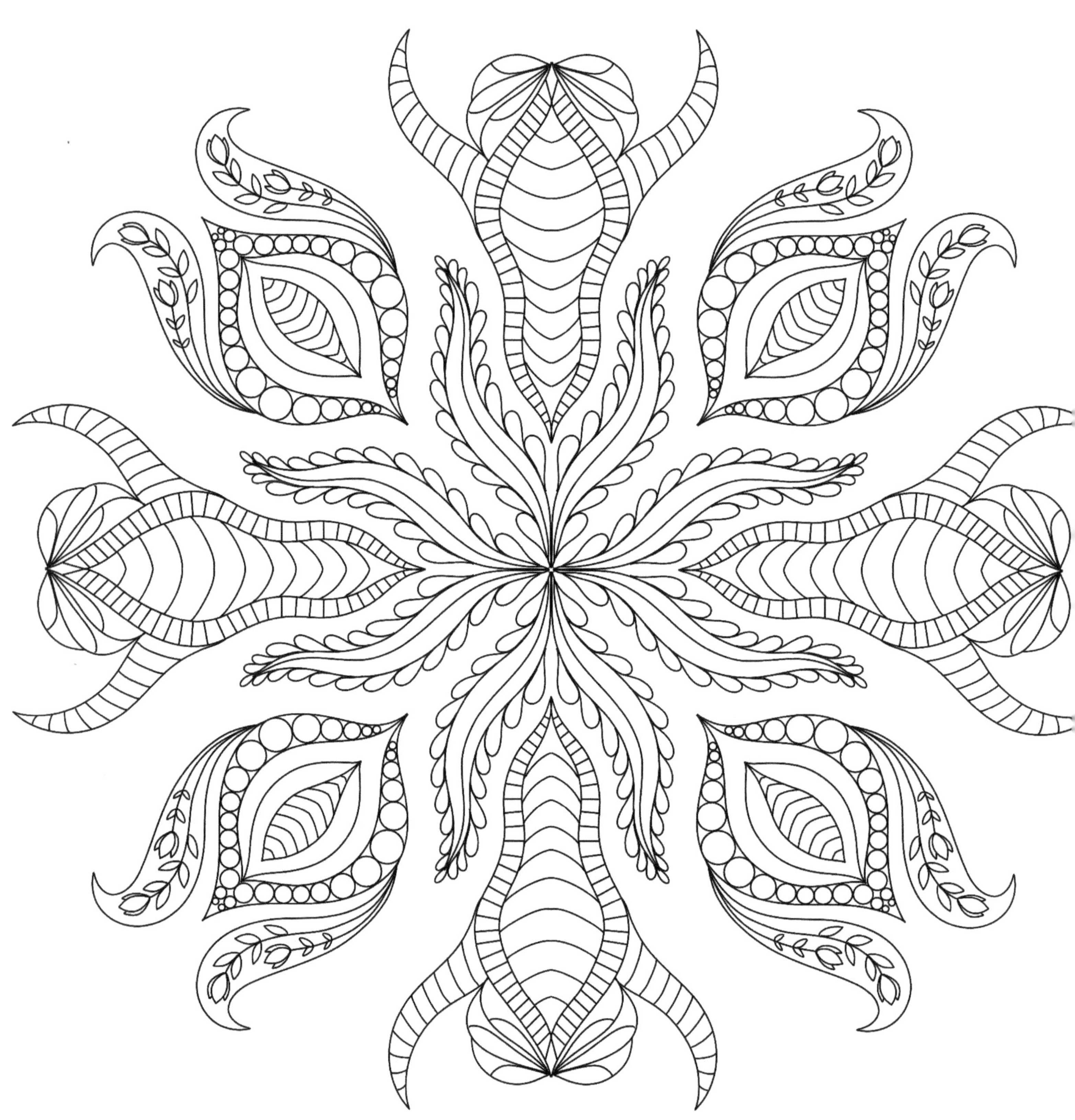

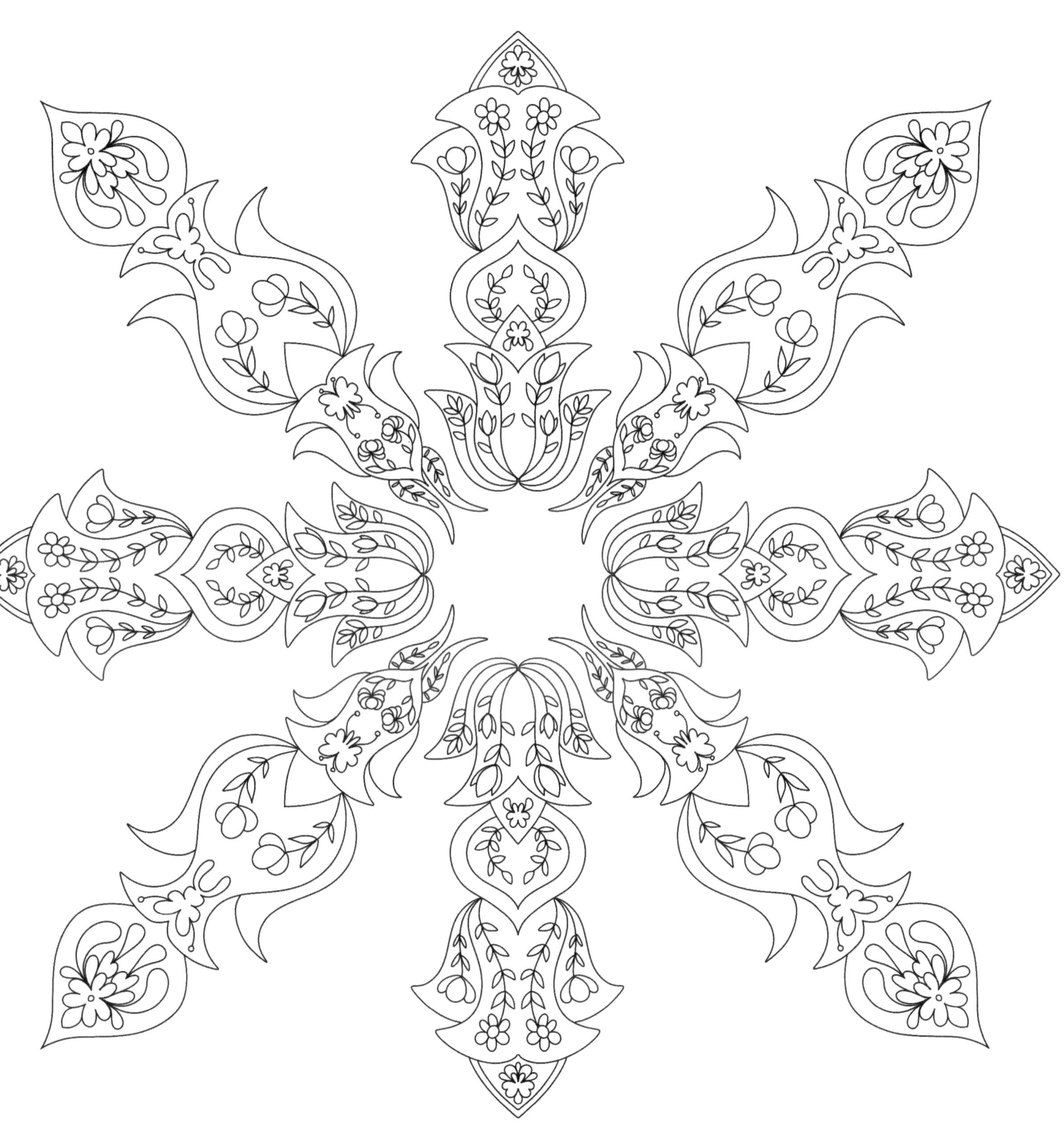

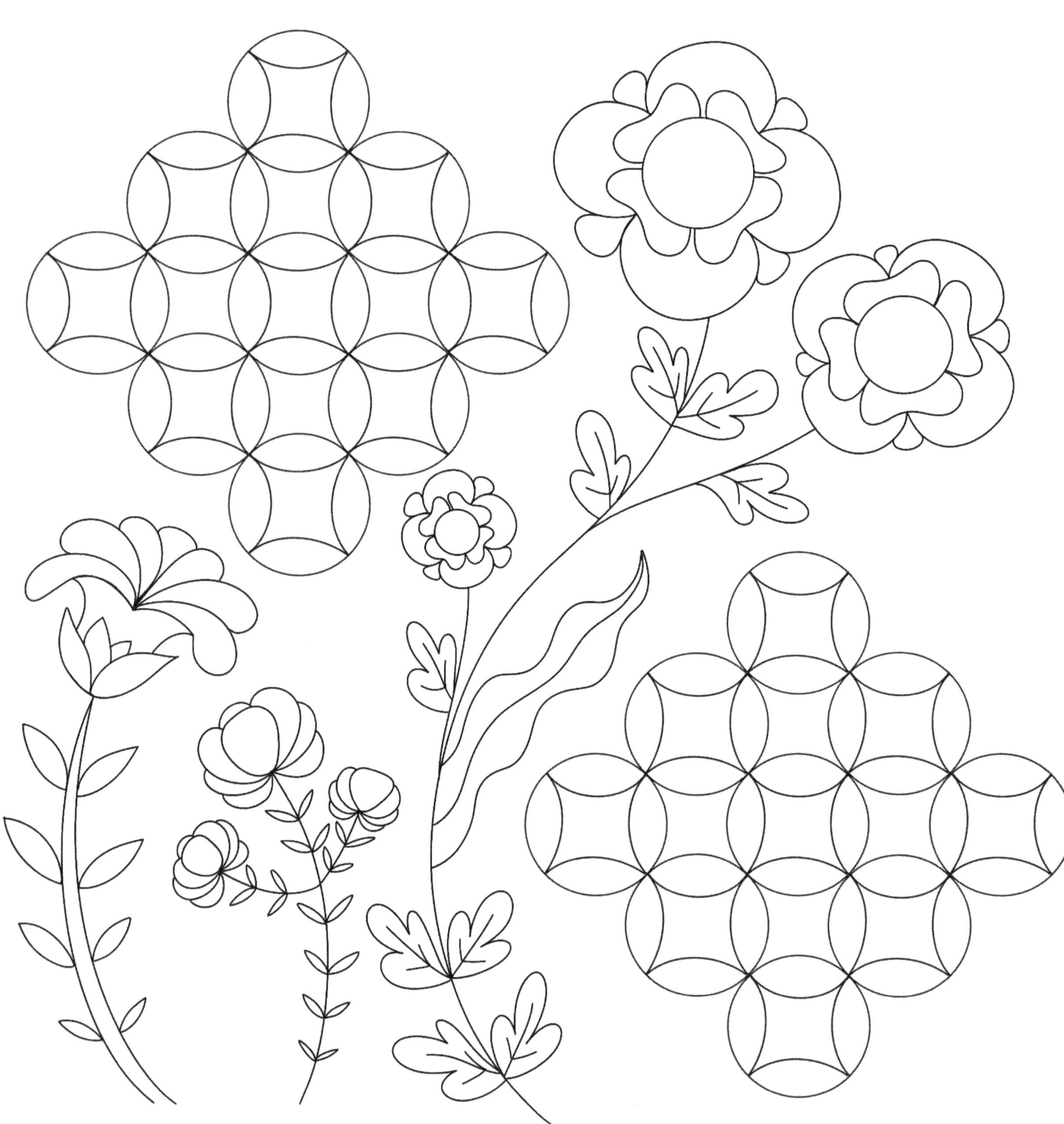

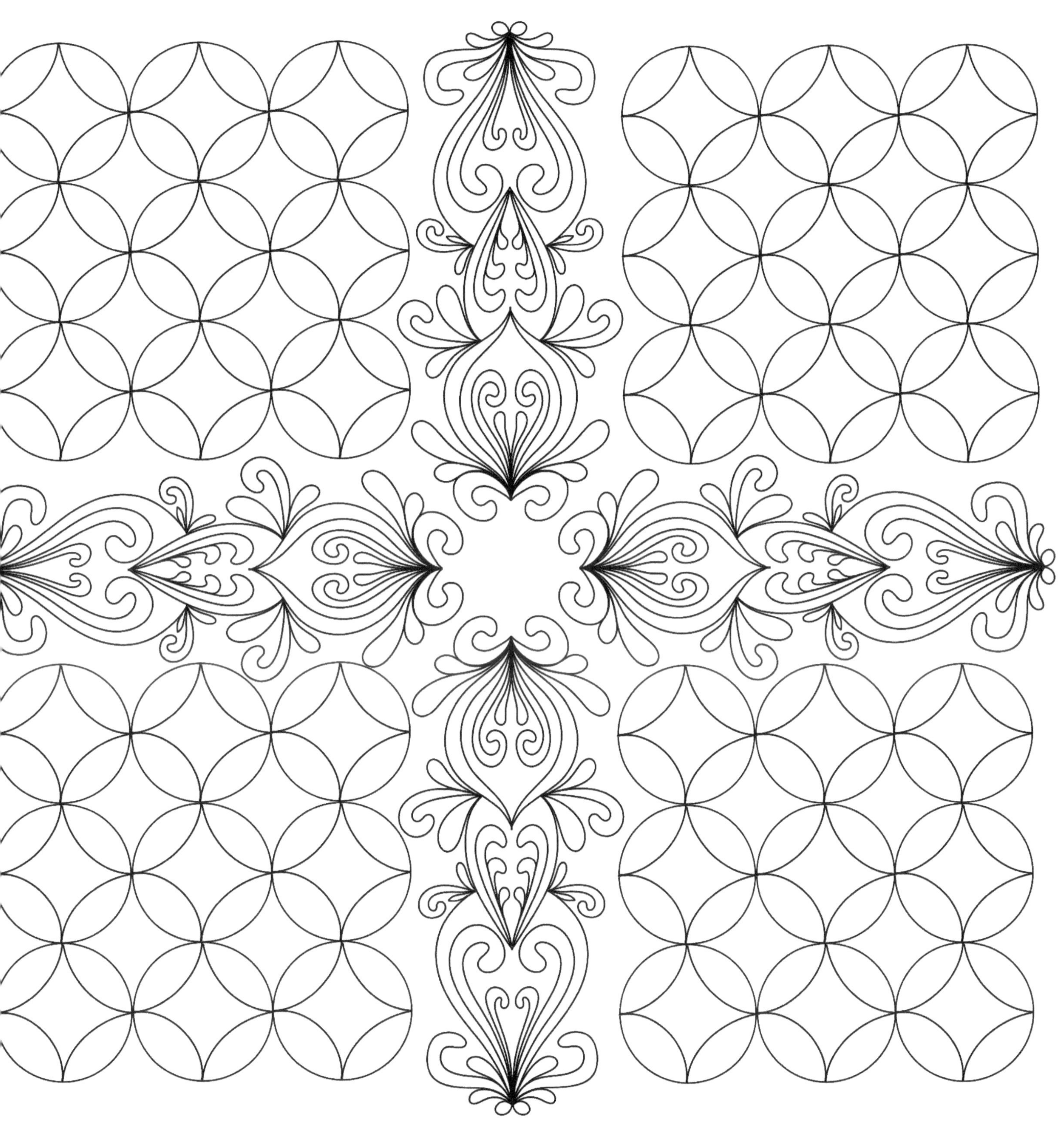

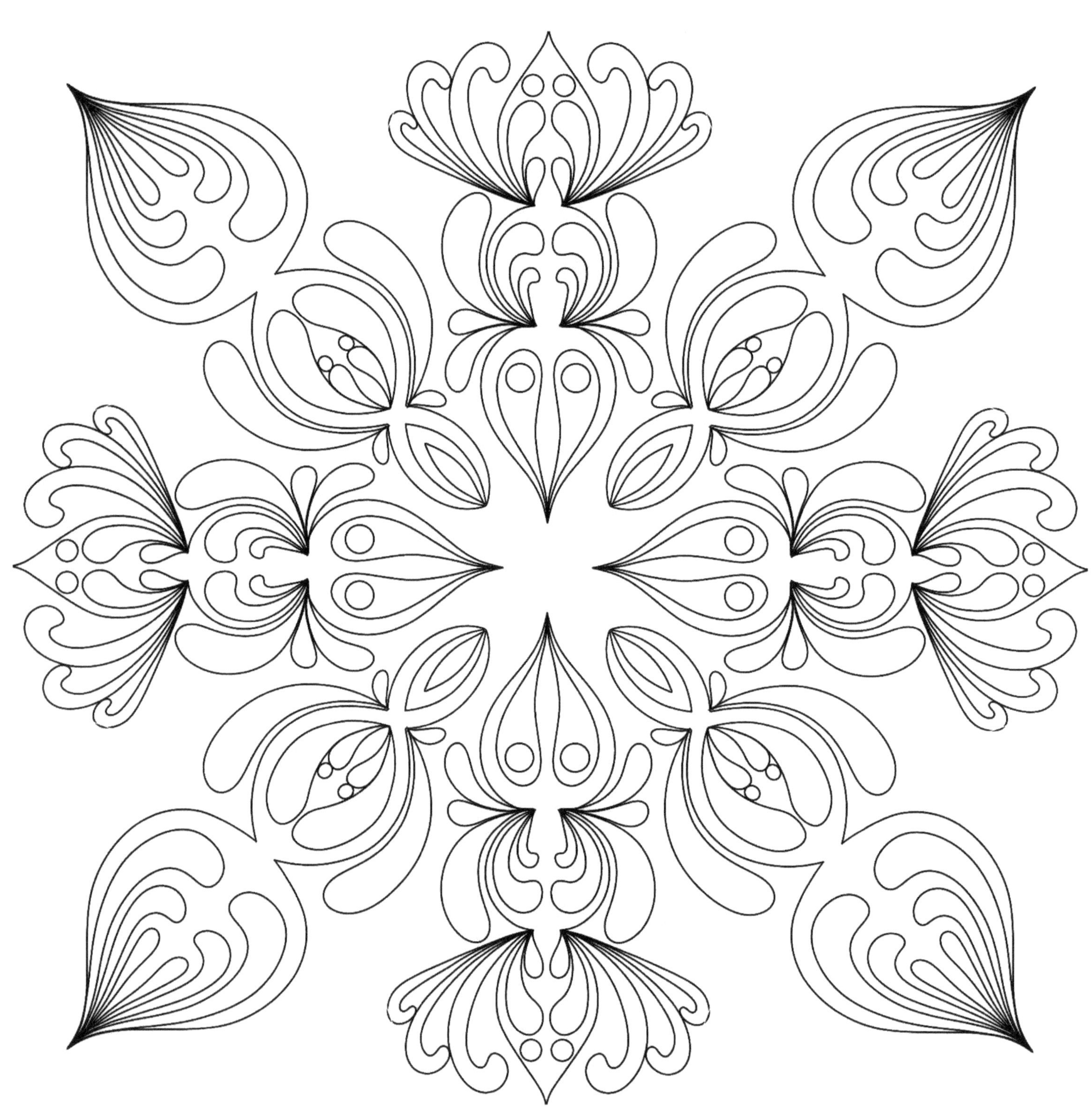

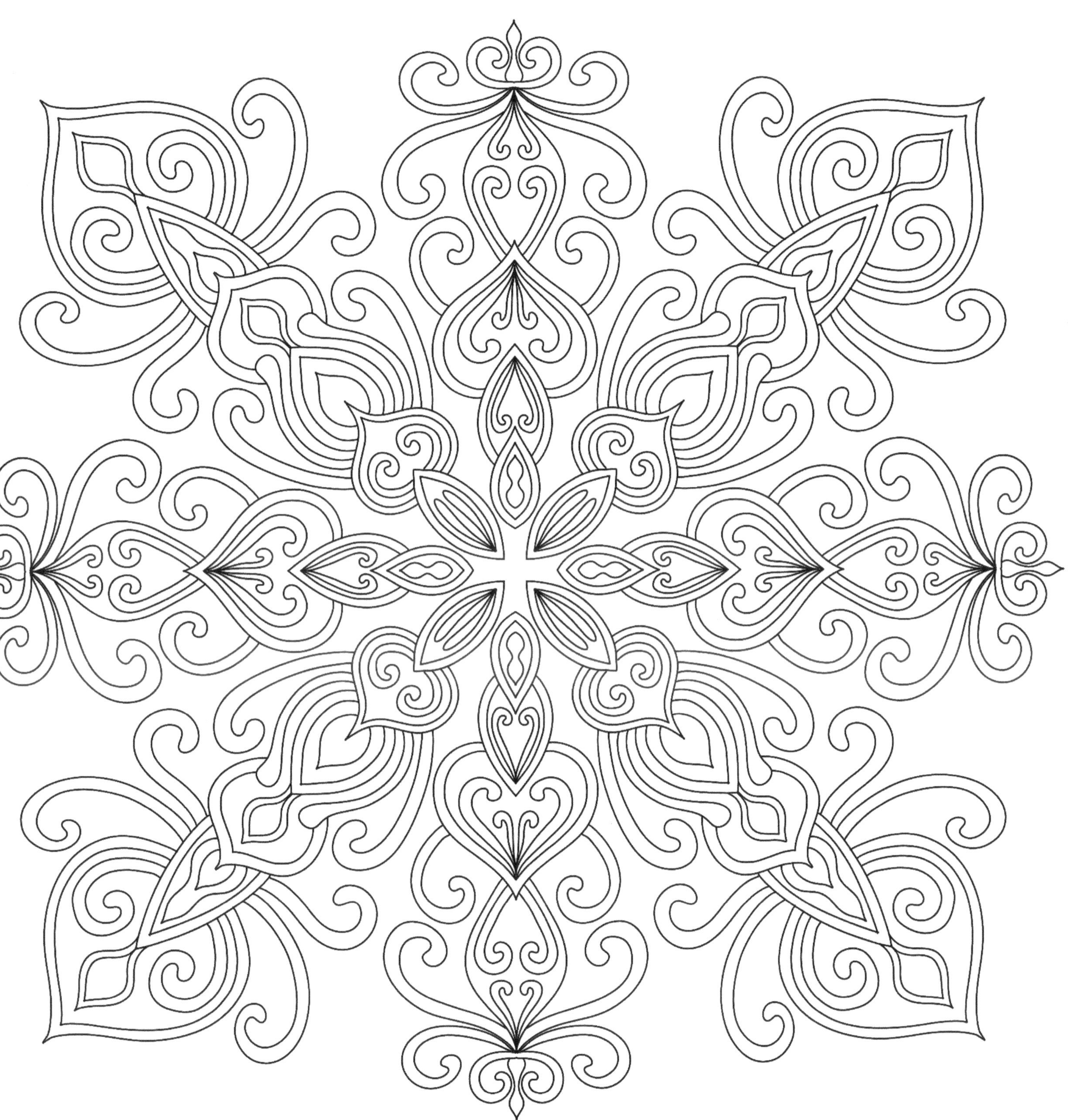

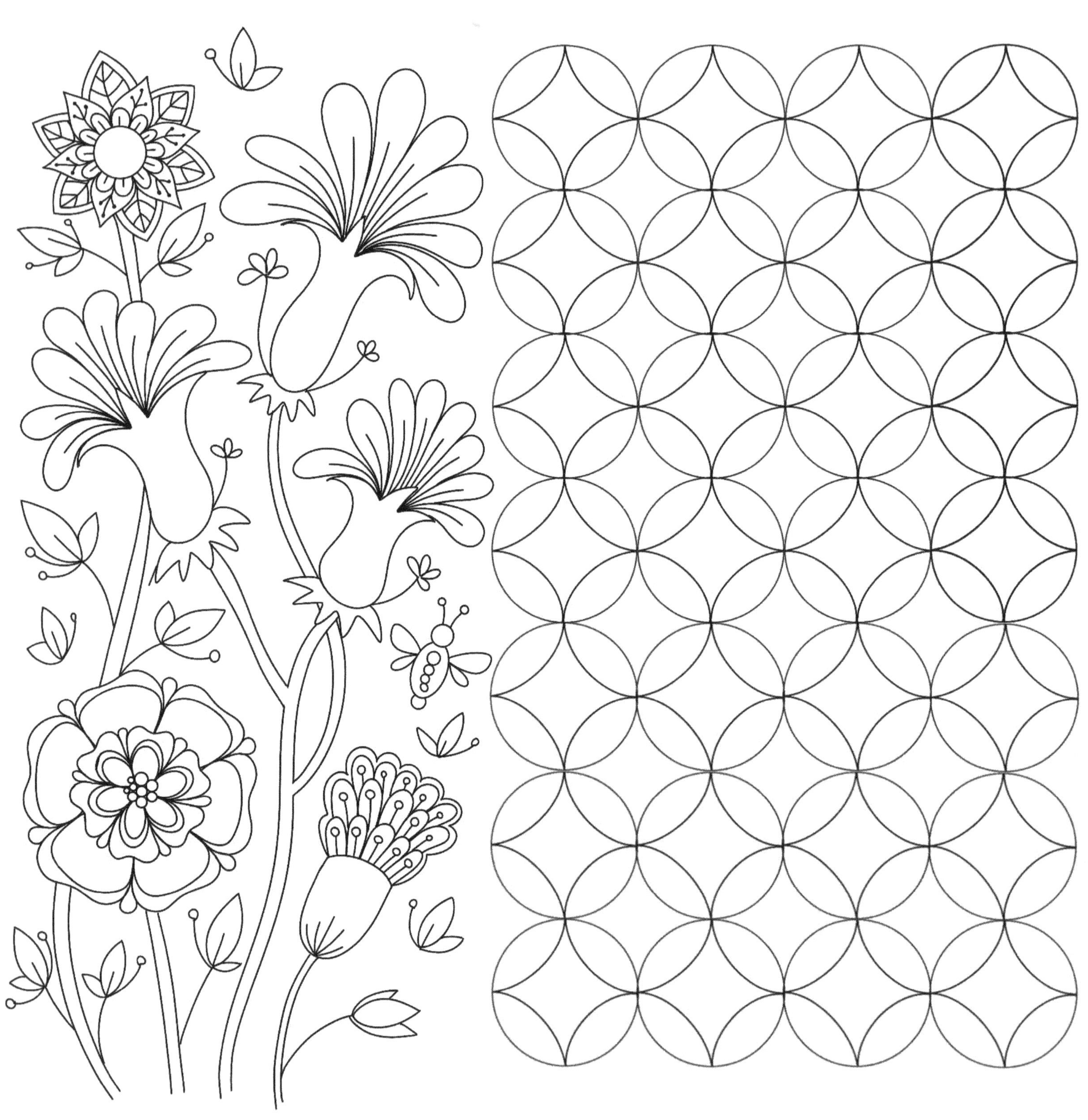

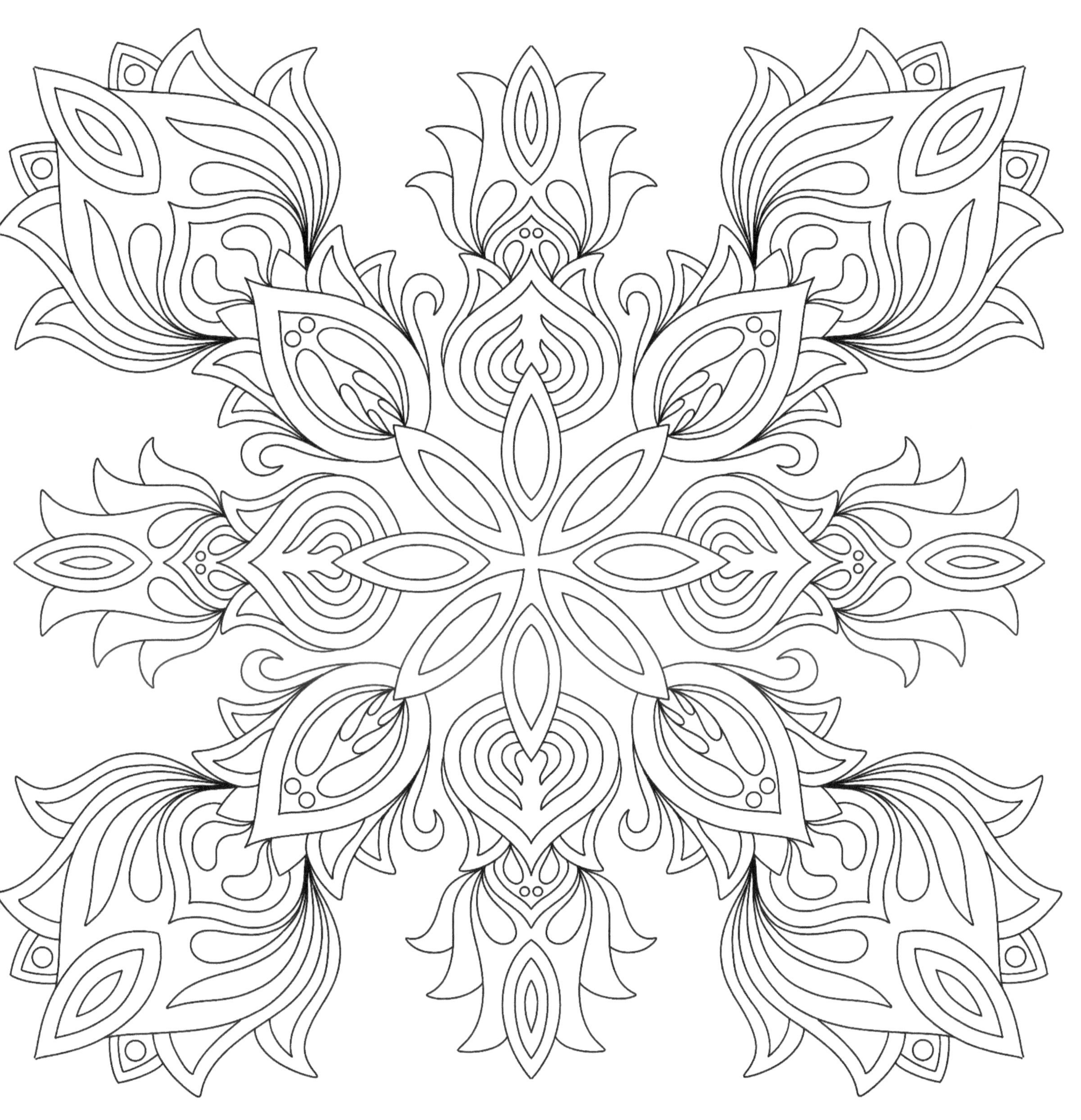

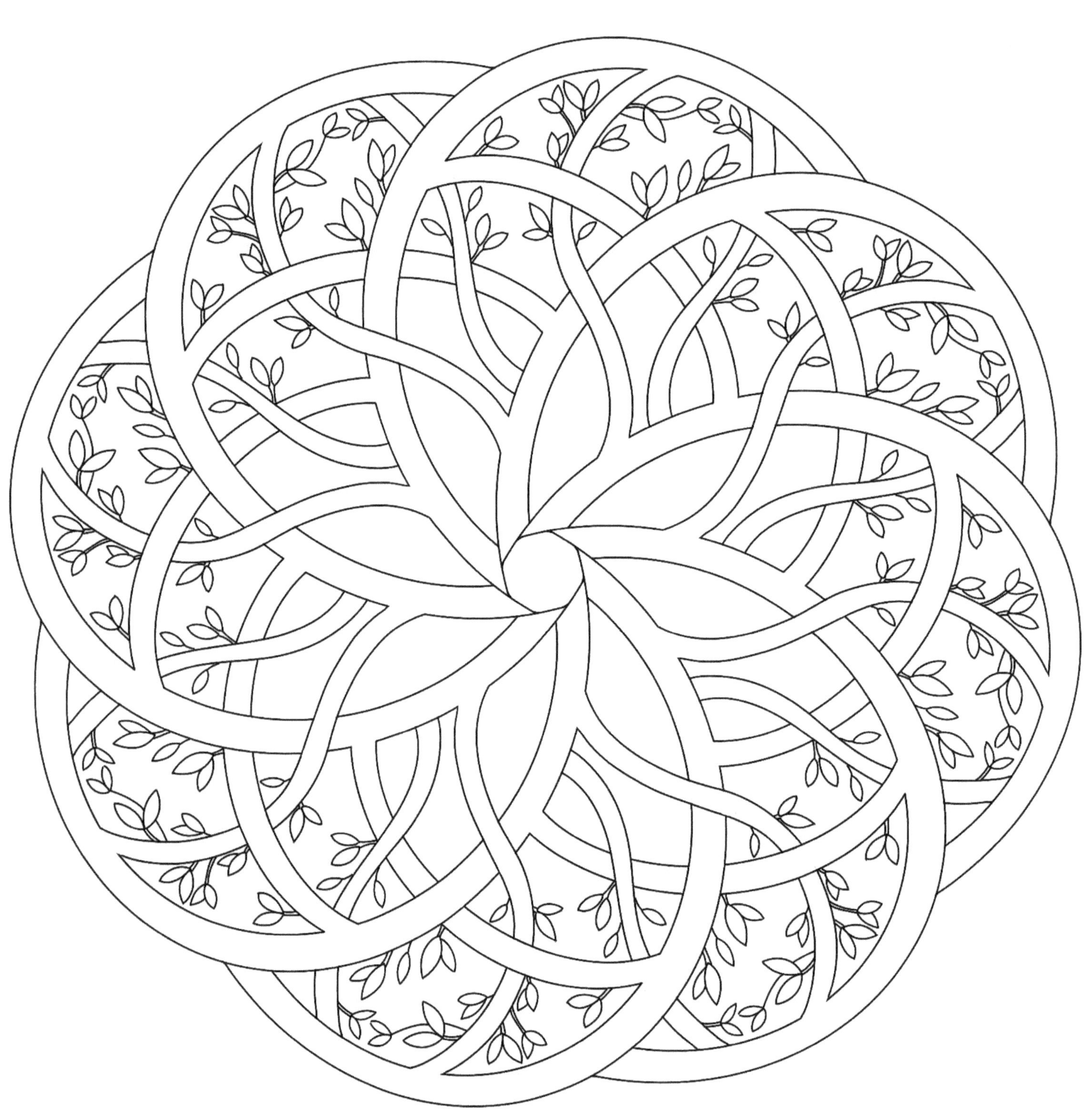

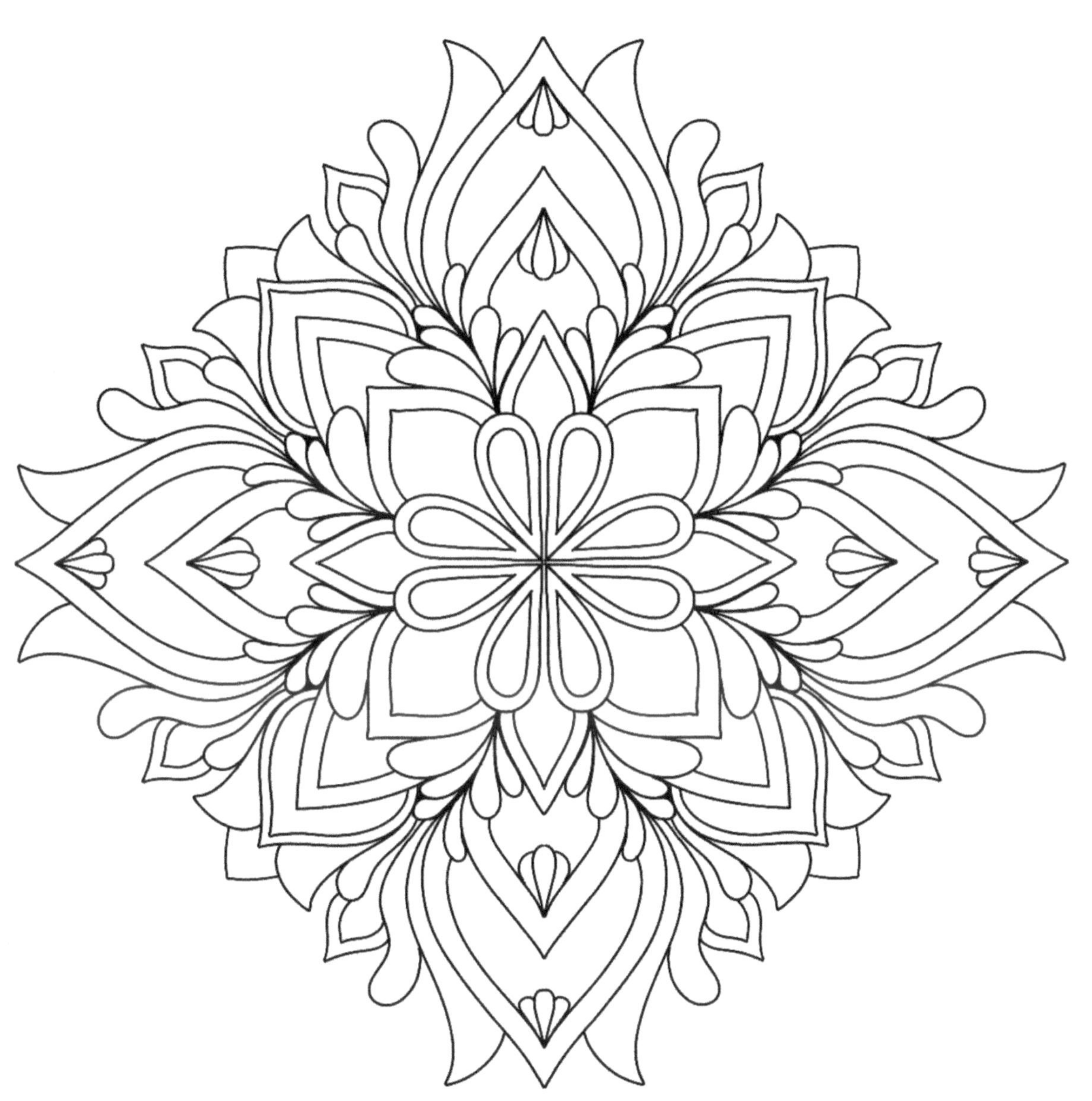

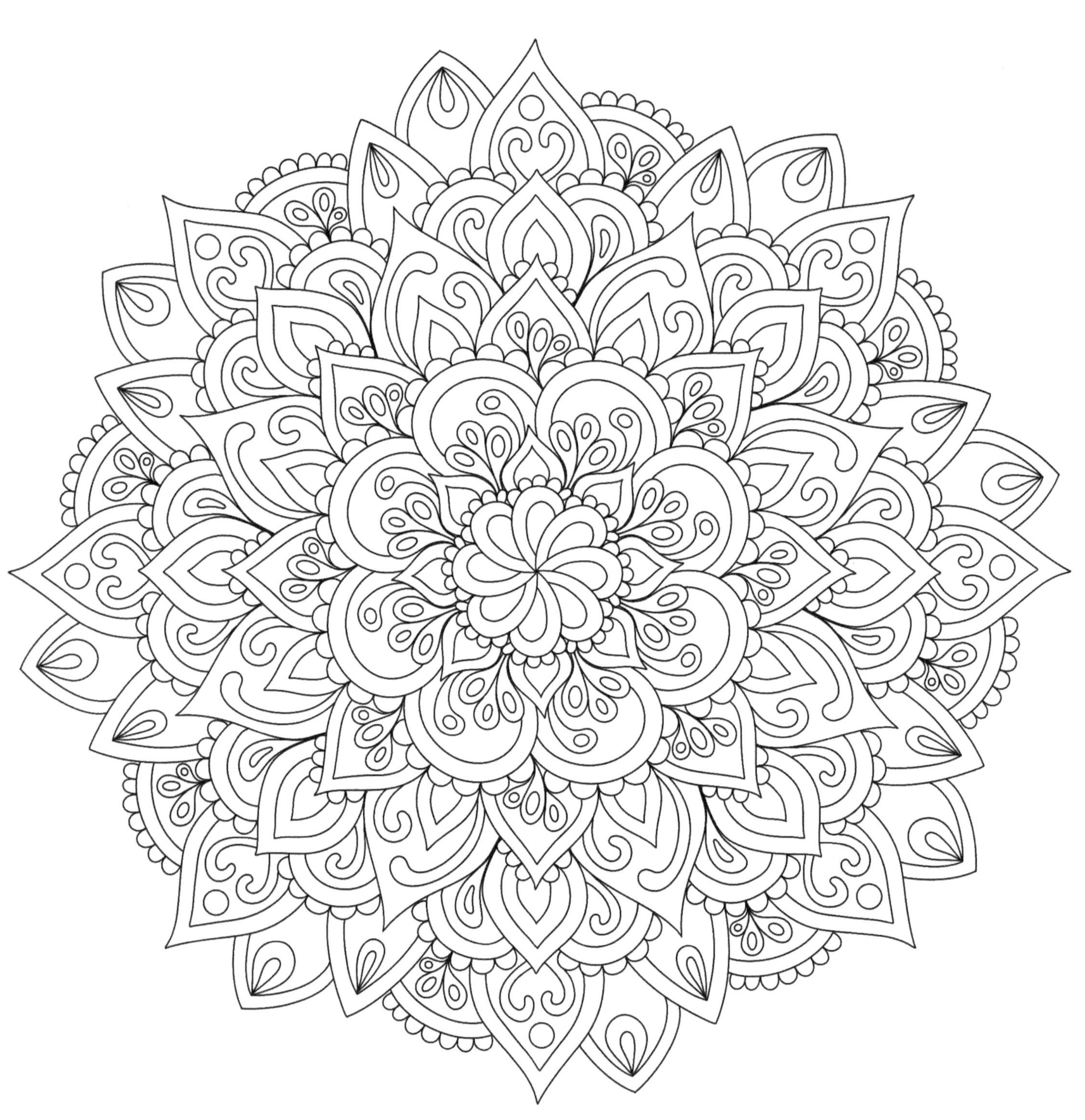

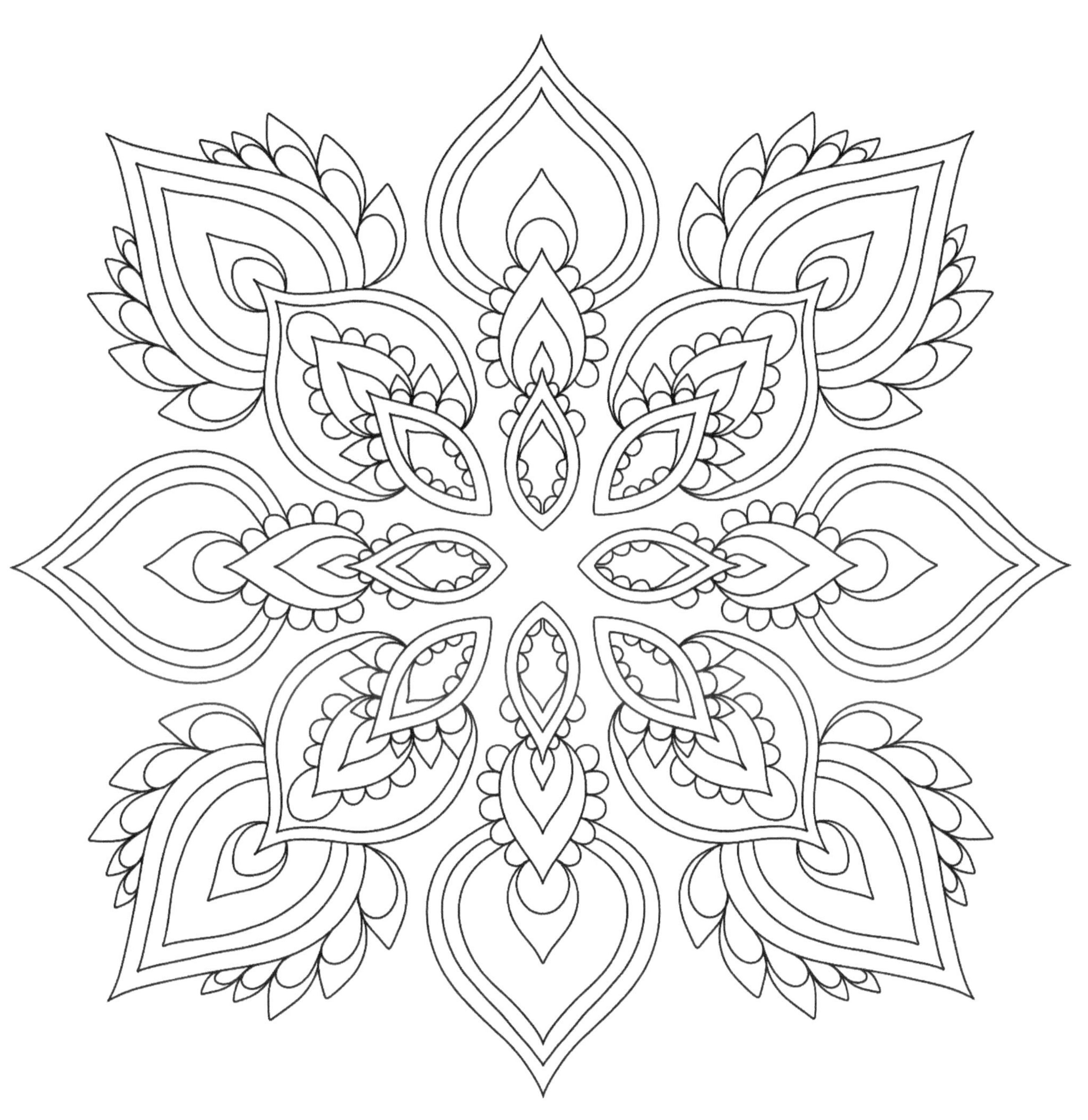

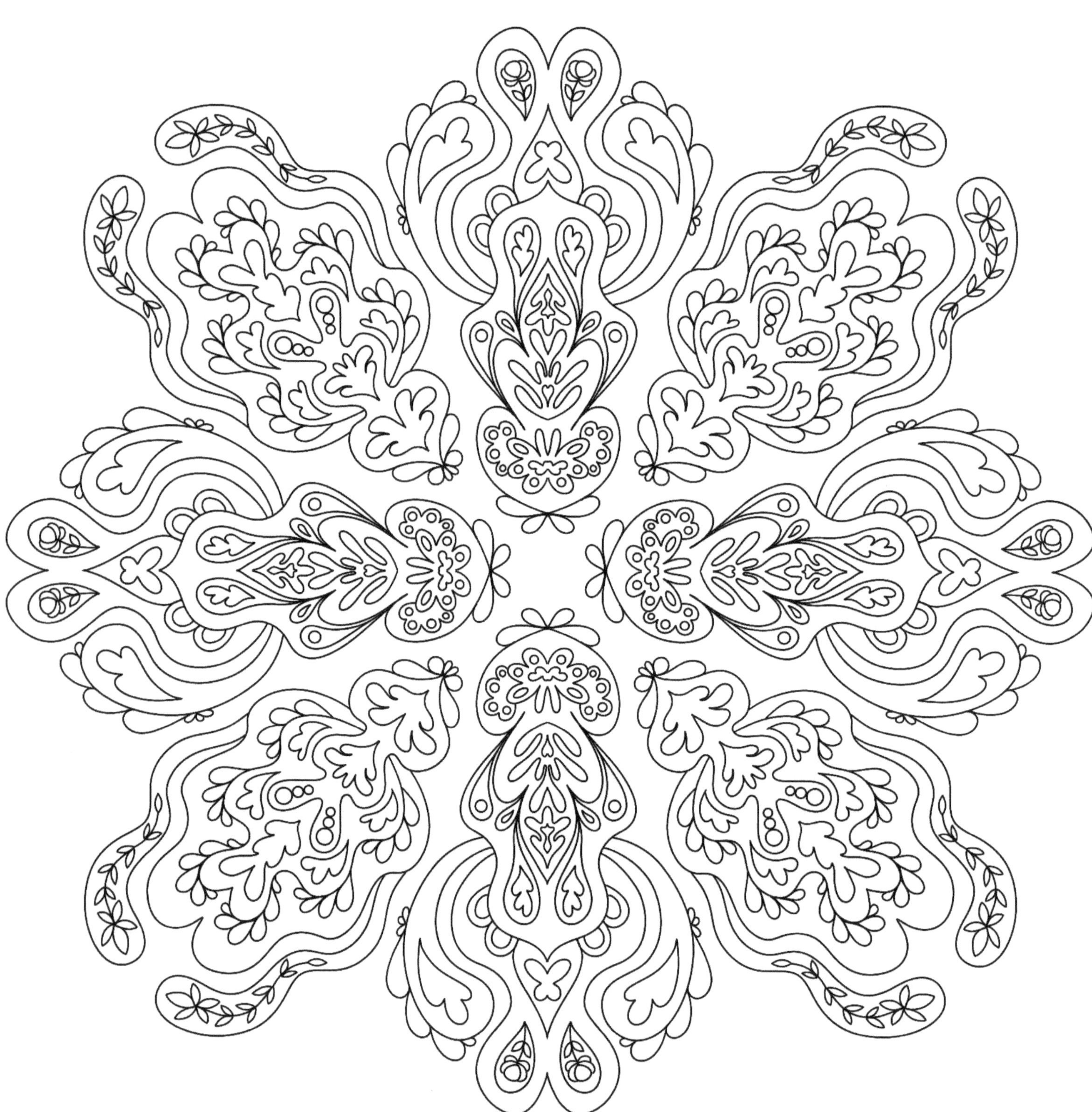

About the Artist

Dina has always been creative, expressing herself mainly through painting and drawing. Seeing the world through creative eyes, she uses art to express her thoughts and feelings. She took every art class available to her inside and outside of school and continues to take art classes and workshops. She holds a Bachelor's of Art in Art with a concentration on graphic design. Her favorite mediums are oil and acrylic painting and drawing using pen and ink, markers, and pencil.

Some of her hobbies include reading, sewing, embroidery, photography, basket weaving, and making her own macramé plant hangers.

She is a houseplant enthusiast and enjoys tending to her inside jungle. She enjoys propagating and growing plants from seeds and is always on the lookout for the next rare plant to add to her collection.

Wherever Dina roamed and called home it was always near the water. Always having a deep appreciation for nature and a special affinity for the water, she loves the ocean and all its creatures.